Raising Thousands (if Not Tens of Thousands) of Dollars with Email
by Madeline Stanionis • Emerson & Church, Publishers • $24.95

After reading the title of this book perhaps you're saying, "Sure, Red Cross and UNICEF can raise tons of money with email, but my agency isn't a brand name. You're telling me I can do the same!?"

Well, no. Author Madeline Stanionis is President of Donordigital, not Pollyanna. But what she is saying is that you can have surprising success if you approach email fundraising with a measure of intelligence and creativity.

Generously dispensing advice and insider tips, Stanionis reveals precisely what you need to do, step by step, to raise substantial money with email.

Raising $1,000 Gifts by Mail
by Mal Warwick • Emerson & Church, Publishers • $24.95

Whoever heard of raising $1,000 gifts (not to mention $3,000, $4,000, and $5,000 gifts) by mail? That's the realm of personal solicitation, right? Not exclusively, says Mal Warwick in his book. *Raising $1,000 Gifts by Mail.*

With carefully selected examples and illustrations, Warwick shows you how to succeed with high dollar mail, walking you step by step through the process of identifying your prospects, crafting the right letter, the right brochure, the right response device, and the right envelope.

Attracting the Attention Your Cause Deserves
by Joseph Barbato • Emerson & Church, Publishers • $24.95

Think of *Attracting the Attention Your Cause Deserves* as a "Trade Secrets Revealed" book, one allowing you to accomplish three key objectives for your cause: greater visibility, a broader constituency, and more money raised

With more than a million nonprofit organizations in existence, there's a lot of noise out there. Shouting won't get you noticed – everybody's doing that. And everybody's tuning it out.

What *will* attract attention is following Joseph Barbato's field-tested advice. Take his insider wisdom to heart. It spills over every single page of this groundbreaking book.

The Mercifully Brief, Real World Guide to ...

Raising More Money With Newsletters Than You Ever Thought Possible

Emerson & Church
Real World Guides

First printed September 2005

10 9 8 7 6 5 4 3 2

Printed in the United States of America

This text is printed on acid-free paper.

Emerson & Church, Publishers
P.O. Box 338, Medfield, MA 02052
Tel. 508-359-0019
Faxx 508-359-2703
www.emersonandchurch.com

Library of Congress Cataloging-in-Publication Data

Ahern, Tom.
  The mercifully brief, real world guide to raising more money with news-letters than you ever thought possible / Tom Ahern.
      p. cm.
  Includes index.
  ISBN 1-889102-07-5 (pbk. : alk. paper)
  1. Direct-mail fund raising. 2. Nonprofit organizations--Finance. I. Title.
  HV41.2.A44 2005
  658.15'224--dc22
                                        2005019774

The Mercifully Brief,
Real World Guide to ...

Raising More Money With Newsletters Than You Ever Thought Possible

TOM AHERN

Emerson
& Church
PUBLISHERS

ABOUT THE AUTHOR

Tom Ahern is recognized as one of North America's top authorities on nonprofit communications. He began presenting his top-rated Love Thy Reader workshops at fundraising conferences in 1999.

Since then he has introduced thousands of fundraisers in the U.S., Canada and Europe to the principles of reader psychology, writing, and graphic design that make donor communications highly engaging and successful.

He founded his consulting practice in 1990. His firm specializes in capital campaign case statements, nonprofit communications audits, direct mail, and donor newsletters. His efforts have won three prestigious IABC Gold Quill awards, given each year to the best communications work worldwide.

Ahern is also an award-winning magazine journalist, for articles on health and social justice issues. He has his MA and BA in English from Brown University, and a Certificate in Advertising Art from the RI School of Design. His offices are in Rhode Island and France.

For Simone, who kissed me to life

CONTENTS

1 You *can* do a great donor newsletter   11

2 Why you need a donor newsletter   13

3 These seven flaws are killing you   15

4 Why try so hard? You are an intrusion   17

5 What donors really care about   19

6 A word on donor (dis)loyalty   22

7 Readers have four personalities   24

8 The four personalities go to a seminar   26

9 Your Inner Amiable   28

10 Your Inner Expressive   30

11 Your Inner Skeptic   32

12 Your Inner Bottom-Liner   34

13 Fatal Flaw No. 1: Failing the "You" test   36

14 Fatal Flaw No. 2: Lacking emotional triggers   39

15 Fatal Flaw No. 3: No news is not good news   42

16 The special language of "News-speak"   44

17 What is news?   47

18   Making news out of thin air   49

19   Recurring themes   52

20   What a front page is for   55

21   How to write news stories: The Inverted Pyramid   57

22   How to write news stores: Start with an anecdote   59

23   Fatal Flaw No. 4: Hogging the credit   62

24   Fatal Flaw No. 5: Expecting people to read deep   64

25   The browser level   65

26   The bouncing eye   67

27   Eliminate gratuitous visual labor   69

28   Pull-quotes bring your buried treasures to light   73

29   Use subheads to break up columns of dense text   76

30   The AP (Associated Press) formula for captions   79

31   Your column width can slow or speed reading   81

32   Lower the grade level of your writing   83

33   Fatal Flaw No. 6: Non- or feeble headlines   86

34   Case study: Hospital headline aims, misses   89

35   How to write great headlines   91

36   Case study: Foundation headline looks right, all wrong   94

37   Fatal Flaw No. 7: Stat crazy, anecdote light   97

38   Tips on using statistics well   98

39   Anecdotes vs. stats   102

40   How often should we mail? Scheduling and frequency   104

41   An easy alternative: The newsy-letter   106

42   E-newsletters   108

43   How should it look? Domain Group's proven formula   112

44   My closing pep talk   114

APPENDIX

ACKNOWLEDGMENTS

ABOUT THE AUTHOR

1

You *Can* Do a Great Donor Newsletter

—❖—

If you're reading this page, you already have the one thing required to publish a great donor newsletter ... and that's a desire to learn.

You don't need a degree in journalism to publish a newsletter that will keep your donors inspired (and generous). You just need a few skills and insights, all covered in the following chapters.

In these pages you'll discover the professional secrets that separate great donor newsletters from the also-rans:

- How to write terrific headlines (and why they're critically important).

- How to spot common graphic design errors that trample your message and drive readers away.

- How a few basic principles of human psychology help you "sell" your story and raise more money.

• What donors *really* want from your newsletter.

One final observation: people often complain about the "drudgery" of putting out a newsletter. And it's true: it can be an irksome chore if you don't have training, a chore that turns to wasted effort when the newsletter doesn't produce the results you'd hoped for.

But a good donor newsletter is surprisingly easy and quick to do, even for novices. Read this book: you'll see. Most important, a good newsletter is its own reward ... in increased support and donor loyalty.

2

Why You Need
a Donor Newsletter

———❖———

In 1995, The Russ Reid Company in conjunction with George Barna of the Barna Research Group, conducted a landmark study of U.S. donors.

This "Heart of the Donor" study quizzed a random sample of 1,164 donors across America about their preferences and opinions.

Among its questions, the study asked donors how the nonprofits they supported could best "keep in touch [and] help you feel more closely connected to and interested in the work of the organization."

Here's what The Russ Reid Company found: "We identified a single stand-out: newsletters. Almost three-quarters of all donors claimed that receiving a regular newsletter would increase their focus upon and interest in an organization."

■ Donors want it. They just don't read it.

And yet Jerry Panas, one of America's most experienced fundraisers, insists, "Every time we survey, donors tell us they don't read the news-letters."

Contradiction? Not really.

Over the past few years, I've reviewed hundreds of newsletters, from nonprofits of all sorts and sizes. Many of these newsletters, maybe most, shared the same, few bad habits. In fact, let's call them what they really are: Fatal Flaws.

Why fatal? Because these flaws *kill* interest.

The truth is, relatively few people will read your newsletter, no matter how good it is. But you'll quickly reduce that already small number to an infinitesimal amount if you fall prey to the fatal flaws.

Worst-case scenario? A deeply flawed newsletter might capture fewer than 10 readers for every thousand copies mailed. Ask yourself: Can you afford those kinds of odds?

3

These Seven Flaws are Killing You

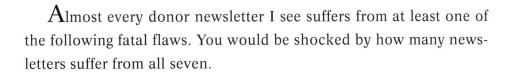

Almost every donor newsletter I see suffers from at least one of the following fatal flaws. You would be shocked by how many newsletters suffer from all seven.

Flaw No. 1

Your newsletter fails the "You Test." I'll explain that simple (but critical) test later. For now just keep in mind that a good donor newsletter is friendly, even intimate, in tone. If you insist instead on an institutional voice, you distance yourself from your readers.

Flaw No. 2

Your newsletter skimps on emotional triggers. You already know that charity starts when you move a heart. In a donor newsletter, tugging the heartstrings is a full-time job.

Flaw No. 3

You claim it's a newsletter (i.e., a bearer of news), but it's really just an excuse to say hi. Here's a dead giveaway: You devote your front page to a ponderous letter "From the desk of" an executive director or board chair.

Beware: a newsletter with no news value is a waste of time and money. And donors are quite demanding: they want very specific kinds of news. Their interest in your organization can quickly wane if you fail to deliver.

Flaw No. 4

Your newsletter isn't "donor-centered." It doesn't make the donor feel needed or wanted. Remember: people don't give *to* your organization. They give *through* your organization, in an effort to change the world. You have to give the donor credit as well as thanks.

Flaw No. 5

The newsletter isn't set up for rapid skimming and browsing. On the contrary, you assume people will read long articles. Here's the harsh truth: most of your audience won't have time to give your newsletter more than a glance. If you bury important information in long articles, most people will miss it.

Flaw No. 6

Your newsletter has weak or dysfunctional headlines. If any of the fatal flaws deserves the title of "Most Deadly," this is it. Headlines have a function: to summarize the key points of the story. Most donor newsletters I've seen fail at that simple task.

Flaw No. 7

It depends far too much on statistics (and far too little on anecdotes) to make your case.

4

Why Try So Hard?
You Are an Intrusion

———❖———

Every day, experts estimate, thousands of messages come at you from every direction (TV, radio, the Internet, your morning newspaper, magazines, billboards, the packages on your shelf, the trucks on the highway, your mail), sent by organizations trying to penetrate your brain and influence your behavior, particularly your spending behavior (which, of course, includes charitable giving).

Your mailbox is one of the busier bees. Direct marketers are nothing if not persistent. (This is probably a good place to note that your donor newsletter is just another piece of direct mail, from the recipient's point of view.)

In desperate self-defense of their privacy and sanity, people have the habit of sorting their mail into three stacks:

Stack No.1 – Stuff they don't dare ignore ... because if they do, something bad will happen. Bills go into this stack.

Stack No. 2 – Stuff they can safely ignore. Catalogs. Direct mail offers. Solicitations from unfamiliar causes. This is the biggest stack by far. This stack goes straight to the trash unread.

Stack No. 3 – Stuff they are somewhat interested in or intrigued by. "Maybe I'd enjoy spending a little time here." Your newsletter's goal is to earn a spot in this stack.

But getting into Stack No. 3 means, first of all, eliminating fatal flaws, the ones I described in the previous chapter. Second, always remember: donors automatically view your newsletter (as they view every other incoming message) as an intrusion, until proven innocent – or, even better, until proven *interesting*.

If your newsletter *is* interesting, though, it will become in time a welcome part of the donor's life, every issue adding another chapter to the ongoing adventure novel, *How My Gifts Saved a Piece of the World*.

5

What Donors
Really Care About

———❖———

I've spoken to dozens of fundraising experts over the years; read their books, their articles, their newsletters, their research; attended their workshops; watched them work their miracles. I have 15 years of experience myself writing fundraising materials.

And this is what I've learned. Donors are principally interested in four things:

- Your accomplishments (How effective is your organization? What did you do with my money? Are you fulfilling the mission I invested in? What are your results?)

- Your vision (What would you do if I gave you *more* money?)

- Recognition (Am I important? Did my help matter? Did I change the world?)

- Your efficiency. Donors will be surprised and delighted to hear that you spend a very small percentage of their gift on administration and fundraising costs. (You do point this out to them, I hope.)

■ Not to, but through

As I mentioned earlier, donors don't give *to* your organization. They give *through* your organization hoping, among other things, to:

- *Fix a problem they worry about.* Afraid your civil liberties are under assault in post-9/11 America? Join the American Civil Liberties Union.

- *Sustain or expand a solution they believe in.* Do you believe effective sex education is one major reason why teen pregnancies are down sharply? Give to Planned Parenthood.

- *Get more of what they like.* Calling all bird lovers: the zoo wants to build a hummingbird aviary, the only one for a thousand miles. Or,

- *Feel like they've made a difference in their community or the world.* ("My support did that? I'm so glad and proud I contributed.")

■ And don't forget to say "Thank you!"

You can't really thank your donors enough. Deep, heartfelt thanks should appear in every issue of your newsletter.

Pretend you are thanking someone who has saved your life, and you'll be striking the right note. Your goal is to convince donors that they are critically, *stupendously*, IRREPLACEABLY important ... and, furthermore, that you depend on their *continued* support.

There's another reason for getting very good at giving thanks: it's an easy way to distinguish your organization from the mob.

Despite all the lip service paid to the importance of thanking donors, surprisingly few charities express much gratitude, studies find. It's a shame and poor practice, but it's a fact - one you should take advantage of.

Thank your donors conspicuously, and you *will* stand out. Which means the next time you send a solicitation letter, those donors are far more likely to remember your organization fondly.

6

A Word on Donor (Dis)loyalty

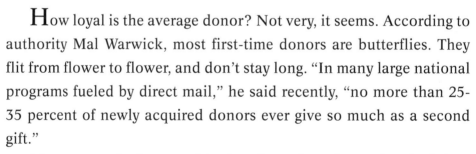

How loyal is the average donor? Not very, it seems. According to authority Mal Warwick, most first-time donors are butterflies. They flit from flower to flower, and don't stay long. "In many large national programs fueled by direct mail," he said recently, "no more than 25-35 percent of newly acquired donors ever give so much as a second gift."

I have more bad news, this time from the *Chronicle of Philanthropy*. Read this and weep: "Public confidence in charitable organizations ... continues to stagnate and shows no signs of recovering [from a 2001 decline], according to a report by the Brookings Institution."

Only 11 percent of Americans think charities do a "very good" job of spending money, said the Brookings report. The other 89 percent have their doubts. In fact, more than one-quarter of Americans believe charities are inept at managing money, according to the report.

Is it any wonder, given these persistent negative attitudes, that American donors are so flighty? Donor loyalty depends to some degree on trust. And donors in general aren't that trusting.

Nor is donor skepticism a peculiarly American phenomenon. In England, researchers asked donors to guess, "What percentage of your gift does your favorite charity spend on fundraising?" British donors speculated that, on average, 65 percent of every gift was spent on fundraising activities, leaving just 35 percent to spend on programs.

You're probably protesting, "But we spend more than 80 percent on programs!" That may be true, but your donors don't know it. Think back: When *was* the last time your newsletter talked about how you spend your money?

Bruce Campbell, a leading researcher into donor attitudes and behavior, finds that "information regarding how finances are used" is among donors' top concerns. This is their perennial question: "Did you spend my money on paper clips and business lunches? Or did you change the world?"

Don't leave your donors guessing. They *will* guess wrong ... and not in your favor. One reason renewal rates, retention rates, and long-term loyalty are all so abysmally low is raging donor skepticism.

7

Readers Have
Four Personalities

When you read a newspaper or newsmagazine or newsletter, different parts of your personality respond to different things.

Sometimes you respond to faces. Sometimes you respond to the excitement of the new. Sometimes an anecdote captures your heart. Sometimes you find the answer to a question that has nagged you. Sometimes you're inspired to act now.

It's as if your head has four sets of ears, each set tuned to a different frequency. I first heard about the "four personality types" in sales training. There's the "Amiable" you, the "Expressive" you, the "Skeptical" you, and the "Bottom-liner" you.

■ Bunk?

You might have already encountered this theory in another form. A half-dozen theories of four-part personalities pound the pavement, looking for converts. The Myers-Briggs test, Holy Writ among Human Resource types, is one. Most are based on the writings of psychologist Carl Jung.

Is it all just pop-psychological bunkum? Perhaps. But even so, it's *useful* bunkum. Speaking to all four personalities gives you four chances to get inside a donor's head; four chances, with every headline and anecdote and photo you publish, to capture the donor's attention.

I guarantee you: Pay attention to all four personality types, and your messages will strike home far more often.

- They will have humanity ... and speak to the Amiable.

- They will have news value ... and speak to the Expressive.

- They will answer objections ... and allay the Skeptic's doubts.

- And they will always remember to tell people exactly what to do next ... and the Bottom-Liner will respond.

But (and I hate to be the bearer of bad news again) many donor newsletters miss these opportunities. In fact, an astonishing number of them *miss all four* chances to score. Which is actually quite a trick when you see how easy it is to do this right.

8

The Four Personalities Go to a Seminar

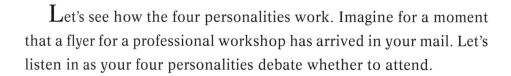

Let's see how the four personalities work. Imagine for a moment that a flyer for a professional workshop has arrived in your mail. Let's listen in as your four personalities debate whether to attend.

• *Your Inner Expressive* exclaims: "Wow! I've never seen this before. And look: it says, 'Secrets revealed.' I'm in! Who knows what I'll learn? Sounds awfully good! Why, this could even change my life!"

• *Your Inner Amiable* smiles: "I'll be around people I like and respect. I'll get to exchange stories and ideas with them. I might even make a new friend!"

• *Your Inner Skeptic counters:* "Whoa. I'm not so sure. Maybe, just maybe, she has something to say. On paper she sounds qualified. But they always do. These things are never as good as advertised. Still

... you never know. It's on Thursday. I'm usually not that busy on Thursday. I don't know. Should I call for more information?" On and on.

It's characteristic of the Skeptic, this inability to decide, a fatalistic suspicion that there really are no good choices. Note, too, skeptics are information junkies. You can never tell them enough. But you can lower their anxiety level by providing testimonials and lots of information.

    • *Your Inner Bottom-Liner concludes:* "Enough. Sounds good. I want to do my job right the first time. She'll tell me how. Does it say if I can pay online?"

9

Your Inner Amiable

Your "Inner Amiable" is that part of you which is glad to see another human face ... which is intrigued by other people ... which responds to a friendly overture.

It's the part of you which empathizes with others' sufferings. "There but for the grace of God go I."

For the Amiable, other humans mean comfort, security, friendship, community, pity, sorrow, compassion ... maybe even a chance to help another and save yourself at the same time.

It's also the part of your personality that responds powerfully whenever you read or hear the word *you*.

Donor newsletters cannot thrive without heaping helpings of Amiable content. In fundraising, it's axiomatic: "People *give* to people." That's not an opinion. It is a powerful and dependable psychological fact. "Human interest" attracts the eye and mind.

If you tell stories (especially micro-stories, a sentence or two long) ... if you use photo portraiture well (eyes particularly) ... if you sow the word *you* throughout your newsletter ... you will force people to pay closer attention.

■ How to speak to the Inner Amiable

To reach the Amiable, use:

- Photos of faces. Close-ups are especially effective. The eyes in photos attract readers' eyes, studies have proved.

- Anecdotes. They don't have to be long, either. A single-sentence squirt of anecdotal information in a photo caption works as well as a novel.

- The word "you" in abundance.

10

Your Inner Expressive

——❖——

Why are newspapers, news shows and newsmagazines so appealing, day after day? Why do our ears perk up when we hear words like "secret" and "confidential"?

Meet the "Expressive You," the part of your personality that is easily excited, that craves hearing about anything new. But be forewarned: it's also the part that is quickly bored. Tell me something I don't know? Oh, goodie. Tell me something I already know? Sorry: been there, done that, see you later.

■ How to speak to the Expressive

To reach the Expressive, use:

- The word "new"

- Words and phrases that promise "secrets revealed." Example: "What doctors *really* say about your chances of surviving cancer."

- Brief, vivid, action-oriented verbs in your headlines: "looms," "sparks," "woos," "stirs." (*See Chapter 16 for more on this topic.*)

11

Your Inner Skeptic

———❖———

The Inner Skeptic, "Skeptical You," is human nature at its most primitive. We're not too trusting. We demand proof. We raise objections.

Good thing, too. You don't think our species became so grotesquely prolific by being gullible, do you? Doubt and fear played - and continue to play - a vital role in species survival.

Be prepared. Any communications - your newsletter, Web site, brochure, and certainly your fundraising appeals - will awaken a Skeptical response in readers, especially in people who don't know you well.

And the skeptical part of your audience comes well stocked with suspicions and doubts (read: misconceptions) about your organization.

How much of every dollar given to a food bank actually ends up feeding the hungry? Isn't that community foundation just an insider's club giving to its friends? Do all the fancy theories behind a charter school truly cause kids to learn better? Zoos are really just "animal prisons" by another name, aren't they?

Your only defense is to answer objections early and often.

■ How to speak to the Skeptic

To comfort the Skeptic, provide:

• Credible testimonials from people who have used your services.

• Lots of background information. Most readers will ignore it, but the Skeptic needs reassurance. If you provide the data, the Skeptic feels better. You don't have to fill your newsletter's precious pages with background information, though. That's what websites are for: "Visit our website for the full report, downloadable in PDF format."

• Frank answers to frequently asked questions (FAQs). Perfect example: "How much of my contribution do you spend on fundraising ... and how much goes to help people?" Don't use your FAQs to push your own agenda. No one ever asks, "How can I give more money to you?" Yet that kind of self-serving faux question peppers charity FAQs.

12

Your Inner Bottom-Liner

The Bottom-Liner is that impatient, finger-drumming part of your brain that mutters, "Okay, okay, I get it. Yes, you're a fine organization doing important work. So, tell me, what are you asking me to do? And please make it fast."

Bottom-Liners need clear instructions and strong calls to action.

Learn to love Bottom-Liners. For one thing, they have the fastest checkbooks in the West.

■ How to speak to the Bottom-Liner

To reach the Bottom-Liner:

• Make every call to action easy to spot. Let's say you have a brochure about bequests that you'd love to send people. Don't bury the offer in the middle of an article. Instead, celebrate your offer inside a big, bold, easy-to-spot box with a big, easy-to-read headline that trumpets, MAKE A BEQUEST ... AND YOU CAN CHANGE THE WORLD FOREVER. YOUR FREE BROCHURE AWAITS!

• Make every call to action easy to do. Convenience matters ... a lot. Convenience and response rates are directly linked. More convenience equals higher response. Less convenience equals lower response.

Think through any action you're asking people to take. Look for obstacles and eliminate them. "Okay, we want our newsletter's readers to sponsor a bike rider in our 100-mile charity race. How easy can we make that? Do they have to send us a check? Or can they give on-line? They can? Great! Let's make a big point of that in the newsletter."

• Make every call to action tightly focused. Ruthlessly pare away the extraneous. Focus on making ONE action happen. If you're pushing a bequest brochure, for instance, stick to that exclusively. Don't muddy the waters by offering at the same time brochures about charitable remainder trusts, unitrusts and so on. Those deserve their own spotlight in a separate offer.

13

Fatal Flaw No. 1: Failing the "You" Test

You.

Who would guess that a pronoun so common and small is in fact among the most powerful words in English? Not internal-combustion-engine powerful, mind you. But atomic powerful, blazing-surface-of-the-sun powerful.

Who would guess that this mere monosyllabic is the most profitable word in fundraising? It's true. Every day, effective use of the word *you* moves mountains of cash into the bank accounts of nonprofit organizations.

How? Why? Because the word *you* is our favorite word. It wields a peculiar superpower: by itself, it can *force* people to pay attention.

You is glue. It really is. It *sticks* the reader to the page. (And, no, the word *we* (*us, ours*) doesn't work the same way. *We* does not have the same emotional intimacy or the "pay attention, I'm talking to you and you alone" power.)

■ You is as personal as newsletters get

Bear in mind that a donor newsletter is just another kind of direct mail. Indeed, it could be argued that it's really a fundraising letter in different guise. After all, your newsletter and your appeal letters share a goal: to bring in gifts.

There is one big difference, though: your ability to personalize.

In direct mail appeals, personalization ("Dear Jane Joyaux" instead of "Dear Friend") increases income. But personalization is next-to-impossible in a printed newsletter.

However, there is one kind of personalization your newsletter can indulge in: unlimited use of the word *you*. Go for it.

■ The "you" test to the rescue

Perform the "you" test on every fundraising piece you write. I do. This test has saved me many times from sending out stuff that was "you-anemic."

The "you" test is simplicity itself.

Get out a red pen. Circle each instance where you have used the word *you* or any variation thereof (*yours, yourself, you're*).

Then look. Are there red circles everywhere you look, at the top, at the bottom, in the middle, and *especially* in your headlines? If so, you've passed the "you" test with flying colors.

Here's a terrific example of a *you*-rich headline from the Rhode Island Community Food Bank newsletter:

If You Had to Choose Between Paying Your Bills and Feeding Your Children, What Would You Do?

On the next page is an example of a "Letter from the Director's Desk" that aces the "you" test:

Letter that Passes the "You Test"

Director's Desk

It's that time of year again.

I'll be sending you a personal letter soon to ask you to renew your gift.

>> But there's a man down in Texas who prays you won't give us a dime.

In fact, this Texan's goal in life is to close every Family Planning office in our state. And he hopes you'll join him in his crusade, by withholding your support.

Meet Mark Crutcher, of Denton, Texas.

He's somebody you've probably never heard of.

But I think it's important that you know your enemy.

Because, if Mark Crutcher has his way, then yours will be the last generation of women in our state who have ready access to good reproductive health care and effective family planning.

Mark Crutcher and his busy organization, Life Dynamics, Inc, based in Denton, Texas, are determined to take away everything your gift supports.

Contraceptives, particularly emergency contraception, one of our leading services: GONE. Sexual education: GONE. Our HIV testing in the inner cities, where HIV infection is a rising epidemic among young African-American women: GONE.

And of course any reproductive choice: GONE. That goes without saying. The last thing he wants is for women like you and me to have control over our own bodies.

14

Fatal Flaw No. 2: Lacking Emotional Triggers

❖

Direct mail is without doubt the most heavily tested communications medium in the world. Here in America, over the decades, fundraisers and other marketers have spent untold billions of dollars on direct mail tests.

Serious direct mailers (i.e., the ones that make good money at it) see every catalog, fundraising solicitation, and special offer as an opportunity to increase response and income, by testing something.

Why should you care? Because over these decades of testing, the direct mail industry has reached a consensus on what motivates people to respond to fundraising appeals.

Emotion. Seven emotions actually: fear, guilt, greed, exclusivity, anger, salvation, and flattery.

■ Negative and positive emotions work together

You might be thinking, "But these emotional triggers sound so negative!"

Not really. Every negative emotion has a powerful, positive flipside.

And somewhere between a negative emotion (fear) and a positive emotion (hope, love, faith, duty, compassion, caring) a check gets written or a gift is made online.

Here's a formula that works:

Stir a negative emotion;

Offer relief through a positive emotion;

Then invite the donor to help you right the wrong.

A few examples of this formula:

• "How early can you predict a child's future? A third-grader who can't read well will probably always be poor, studies show. The shame is, it doesn't have to happen. Our programs have poor kids reading well by first grade. We're ready to expand. Are you ready to help?"

• "Well-funded timber interests are cutting Congress down to size. But it's not too late to save America's wilderness. The fate of our last virgin forests now depends on you: your voice, your love of all things natural ... and your strong support."

• "If you care about your personal freedom, there are seven new federal laws you're going to hate. The good news: There's still time to reverse them ... if you'll stand with us today."

■ Emotional triggers battle inertia

People encountering the notion of emotional triggers for the first time sometimes object: "This is just a form of manipulation. I don't like being manipulated. And I certainly don't want to manipulate anyone else, no matter how worthy my cause."

A) Get over it. Your job is to raise money.

B) Using the emotions knowingly is *not* manipulation. People already have these emotions: fear, anger and so forth. What your organization offers is a productive way to discharge (i.e., relieve, do something about) powerful emotions that pre-exist in (and trouble) the donor.

Let's be clear: the biggest problem you'll encounter in fundraising isn't that someone falls prey to your magical, Svengali-like powers of persuasion. Your biggest problem will always be inertia.

INERTIA!!! It's the most powerful force on earth, more powerful than gravity. You get up on your soapbox, make your plea, and no one does a thing. That's real life. Most of the people you're trying to move will not act.

But when you use emotions wisely you can overcome some (never all) of that inertia. One more comment (and it's tough love): A working knowledge of emotional triggers is a prerequisite in effective communications. If you want to succeed at a professional level, you *have* to understand this stuff.

15

Fatal Flaw No. 3: No News is Not Good News

———❖———

Howard Luck Gossage, an advertising legend, observed: "The fact of the matter is that nobody reads ads. People read what interests them; and sometimes it's an ad." And sometimes it's a headline or an article in your newsletter.

The key word is *interest*. This is a central principle of communications: people only read what interests them. Donors aren't *obliged* to read your newsletter, after all. You have to interest them anew in every issue.

Bear in mind, when you call something a "newsletter," you're making a promise. The promise is this: that you will deliver news of special interest to your particular readers. If those readers are donors, they will (in exchange for your organization's interesting news) pay attention, be inspired, remain loyal, and support your cause with money and time.

Interesting donor newsletters have a few things in common:

• They deliver the right kinds of news. In donor newsletters, the dominant stories should be about your organization's accomplishments, vision, needs, and operational efficiency ... laced with plenty of thanks and recognition.

In fact, if you make the donor the hero ("Here's how we changed the world *thanks to your contribution...*"), you will almost certainly raise more money. A lot more, I'd wager.

• They speed the reader through the news, with effective headlines and other reader conveniences, all of them easy to spot and quick to absorb. They do not bury key messages and information in long articles.

People will not read every word you write. Not even close. Most of your newsletter will remain unread, which means any information in the unread parts will remain unknown ... even if your skills as a journalist are Pulitzer-perfect.

• They speak in the voice of news. News writing habitually adds urgency and drama. Without these two, a newspaper or news magazine would soon be out of business. Donor newsletters that habitually lack urgency and drama share that fate: people learn to stop reading them.

16

The Special Language of "News-speak"

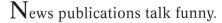

News publications talk funny.

They speak in a way that instantly hooks your Inner Expressive. Through their choice of language, news publications excite that part of your brain that craves drama, struggle, conflict, excitement, power, dynamism, sparkling freshness.

It's the part of your brain that gets all frisky when you hear the word new. The same part, too, that savors secrets, confidential stuff and rumors. "Pssst. Over here."

In the news, words tend to be telegraphic. Concise. Fast. Headlines favor strong, active verbs. "The verb *is* the story," notes one top editor. Here's a list of headline verbs plucked from *The Wall Street Journal*:

Blames	**Embrace**	**Sputters**
Clash	**Looms**	**Surge**
Mauled	**Sowing**	**Devours**

News headlines also favor peril (which is fear, the most easily provoked emotion, crossed with urgency). Consider these headlines from *Maclean's* ("Canada's Weekly Newsmagazine"):

The Web: Waging War on Hackers

What's the story *Maclean's* means to convey? That it's no longer a police action against hackers. Now it's war! Death to cyberpunks!

Climate: The Peril of Warmer Weather

Maclean's hopes to disturb the complacent, who might well wonder: The "peril" of warmer weather? Is it *that* bad? Well, yes! Global warming has turned our planet into a terrarium. Soon there'll be no ice except in your drink.

Europe: Neo-Fascists on the March

Maclean's subliminal warning: Keep an eye on Europe. Last time fascists went on parade, World War II rose from their dust. Can you hear the jackboots now?

■ The verb test

Here is a random list of headline verbs pulled from nonprofit newsletters from across the country:

Administer	Give back	Sets
Awards	Help	Shares
Benefits	Listed	Unifies
Build	Plan	Use
Establishes	Reach	Visits

Compare the nonprofit list to *The Wall Street Journal* list. The difference is striking. The nonprofit list is mostly safe, unexciting, deflated, or stiff. Few of the verbs evoke a scene. They don't stimulate the senses. The *Wall Street Journal* verbs, on the other hand, are highly sensory. You can see them ("devour," "looms," "surge"). You can even *hear* them ("sputters," "clash," "mauled").

Now for the test. Pull out several issues of *your* newsletter. Copy all your headline verbs onto a piece of paper. Do they convey urgency, action, danger, hope, and other strong images? They should. Because that's what it takes to be a newsworthy verb.

17

What is News?

News is anything that 1) Is new and 2) Interests the reader. Here's how it works:

If I am one of your donors, the best news is anything that tells me I backed the right horse, that I'm changing the world because your organization (the one I gave my money and my heart to) is truly, notably effective. That will ALWAYS interest me.

Worry about nothing else.

Your donors need to feel that they are changing the world. That idea pulls an array of emotional triggers.

It feels like salvation. It replaces fear with hope. It replaces anger with a sense of peace and justice. It puts guilt to rest and replaces it with pride in having done the right thing. It makes people believe that their attention and their generosity have mattered, which is the highest (and most remunerative) goal of donor communications.

■ Where do you find news?

If you provide direct service, you get your news from your

program staff, the people working the front lines.

They talk with the people who benefit from your programs. They see the results. They hear the tales. They spot trends emerging in the flesh; and trends are always news.

Learn to be a "news spotter."

- *Look for surprising information*: "Baby spiders thrive in mom's loving care ... unless she's hungry." (Zoo)

- *Look for new angles on existing stories*: "Peeved humming-birds add buzz to aviary visits. Here's a tip: Don't wear red." (Arboretum)

- *Look for emerging problems which donors can help you fix*: "Dust to dust? Not so fast. Proposed painting restoration lab would turn back clock on fading masterpieces." (Museum)

■ Eschew filler

Do donors need to know about your planning retreat and who attended? Doubtful. Do donors care about staff changes? Not much, not really (although to your face they'll be polite).

A donor newsletter packed with this kind of low-wattage stuff has adverse consequences. Basically, you're training your target audience to skip you. The subliminal message that accumulates quickly: "Nothing important here."

18

Making News Out of Thin Air

—❖—

Hey, it happens. Sometimes there's not enough real news to fill an issue. Here are four, fast ways to brew up "news-like" material that donors will find interesting.

■ Fact vs. Myth (a.k.a. the Reality Check)

A "Fact vs. Myth" column uses some of your vast insider knowledge to inform and entertain the donor. Here's an excerpt from the Clean Water Action (MI) newsletter:

> MYTH: Property owners cannot maintain their beaches without getting in trouble with the MI Department of Environmental Quality (MDEQ) or the Army Corps of Engineers (ACOE).

> FACT: [Here are] highlights of what property owners can do without any permits from the ACOE or MDEQ – build sand castles; hand shovel/manually rake dead fish, zebra mussel

shells, trash and dead vegetation; manually bury debris such as dead fish and dead vegetation; bonfire building; temporary tent building and camping by permission of the property owner; and beaching boats and seasonal storage of ice shanties.

The preceding myth-and-fact might or might not interest you, but it was well chosen for its target audience: lakeshore property owners. It delivers useful information about what they can and cannot do. It reduces worry and helps keep people out of trouble with the law. It also positions Clean Water Action as a fair-minded organization that isn't anti-owner, despite occasional disagreements on specific issues.

■ The Update

Updates help position your organization as an authority in your field, something that's probably high on your list of goals. All kinds of support (donor, policymaker, media) gravitate toward a recognized authority.

"West Nile Virus: One Year Later" is a perfect example of the authoritative update. The headline appears on the front cover of *Conservator*, the member magazine of Ducks Unlimited Canada. The mission of Ducks Unlimited Canada: saving wildfowl by preserving wetlands. The news value of this article: the appearance of a deadly mosquito, which adds a surprising downside to the mission of wetlands conservation.

■ The List

"Top Ten ...." "Seven Worst ...." "Three Most ...."

"There's something irresistibly attractive about lists," says Andy Goodman in his newsletter, *Free-range Thinking*. "Whether scratched on paper as reminders of tasks that need to be done today, or etched in stone as moral guidelines" – oh, right, the Ten Commandments –

"lists have a unique way of taking the complex and making it orderly and understandable. The media inundate us with lists – of box office leaders, top performing stocks, sexiest men alive – precisely because editors recognize their consistent appeal."

The National Parks Conservation Association (NPCA) annually releases a list naming the "Ten Most Endangered National Parks." The press loves it. So do NPCA's 300,000 donors and dues-paying members. The list distills NPCA's mission down into one bracing shot of anger and fear, reminding everyone of what's at stake.

■ The "Did You Know?"

Here's an example from the Conservation Law Foundation newsletter:

> "Did you know? On August 15, 2003, as over 100 power plants remained shut down on the second day of the Northeast's massive blackout, visibility increased by as much as 20 miles because the concentration of light-scattering particles caused by sulfur dioxide emissions was reduced by 70 percent."

Donors to the Conservation Law Foundation hope to save New England's environment from further degradation. This particular "Did you know?", posted prominently on the newsletter's front page, reminds donors exactly what they're fighting for and what their gifts hope to achieve: a day when pollution doesn't add a dangerous haze to the very air they breathe.

19

Recurring Themes

——— ❖ ———

In advertising, repetition acts like a hammer, a *lightly tapped* hammer, slowly driving your message home.

The technical term for this is "frequency." How *frequently* can you repeat the same message to the same target audience? The more frequency you can afford in your advertising schedule, the more sales you're likely to make. (Assuming, of course, you've got the rest of your campaign right. Frequency alone can't win the day.)

In your newsletter, "recurring themes" are useful for the very same reason: because repetition works. What is a recurring theme? Simply any theme you repeat in every issue, either blatantly or between the lines.

A positioning statement or tagline is in essence a recurring theme. In 1972, the United Negro College Fund launched a public awareness campaign with the tagline, "A mind is a terrible thing to waste." Today that tagline is still hard at work, moving donors to invest in the transforming power of a college education.

■ How to pick your themes

What qualifies as a good recurring theme? For a donor newsletter, any message that's vital to your fundraising success.

Southcoast, a community hospital group in Massachusetts, developed three recurring themes for its newsletter.

1) "We're much better than you might imagine. You can trust us to give you and your family great medical care right here in your own community. So we are worthy of your support."

2) "We're currently accomplishing worthwhile things with your money. Your gifts make these wonderful things possible. Your gifts change the world you care about and help fix key local health problems."

3) "We're planning even greater things, with your help. The best is yet to come. We continue to need your support. We're not going away."

Please note: Southcoast never used these actual words. Rather, these were the key messages Southcoast wished to convey.

You'll spot some familiar faces in the Southcoast themes: *accomplishment reporting* (theme two) and *vision* (theme three). In fact, the second and third themes, with minor adjustments, would suit almost any organization.

The first theme – "We're much better than you might imagine." – emerged from focus groups, where participants voiced strong doubts about the quality of care they could expect at a local hospital ... especially with Boston, home to many world-class medical institutions, a 45-minute drive away.

Since Southcoast in fact offers *superb* medical care including specialties in advanced areas such as cardiac surgery (and of course recruits its doctors from those same top-ranked Boston institutions), these lingering suspicions about "the locals" were just plain wrong.

Misperceptions like these can be a serious impediment in fundraising. Prospects won't be inspired to give that first gift, and nominal donors won't be inspired to increase their giving, if your organization is seen as just an also-ran.

So how does Southcoast put its themes to work in its donor newsletter? A typical example was a cover story with a full-page photo of a young man holding a basketball. The story bore this headline:

"I'm Grateful to be Alive" – How great medical care close to home saved Brian DeCosta's life

20

What a Front Page is for

Imagine if your daily newspaper devoted its front page to stories that didn't matter, instead of the leading news. You'd think they were incompetent. And you'd soon be reading something else.

Yet many donor newsletters suffer from a painful malady called "uncertain priorities syndrome." The chief symptom: leading with unimportant stuff, stuff that's neither news nor important to the donor.

As they say: You never get a second chance to make a first impression. Waste your most important real estate – the front page – on stuff that doesn't matter to your donors, and you'll quickly train them to ignore your publication.

As I mentioned in chapter five, donors are interested in what you did with their money (how you advanced the mission), what you *could* do with their money (your vision of the great things you could do), and whether their money mattered ("Thanks, donors, for a job well done!").

They are *not* likely to find much interest in yet another yawn-inducing essay "From the Executive Director's Desk." Please note: I'm not suggesting a ban on "From the Desk of..." columns. They have their place. Usually, though, it's not on the front page.

I know of one exception: Pastor John.

■ How Pastor John made money

In 2001, when we met, Pastor John (John R. Bohnsack) was executive director of the Community Emergency Service in Minneapolis, MN.

His humble, compassionate, and uplifting "Director's Discourse" columns filled every front page of the organization's monthly newsletter.

In a simple, conversational style, he told stories about people who needed help. He talked about how easy it was to change a life. He used the magic word *you* over and over. He called his readers "friend" and meant it.

Pastor John used emotional triggers like greed, salvation, and duty quite openly: "God does seem to find ways of returning tenfold and sometimes even one-hundredfold to those who reach out in faith and give through this ministry to folks whose spirits have been drenched by catastrophe."

And it worked. His "Director's Discourse" inspired an outpouring of money, thousands of dollars a month, to help the city's hungry and homeless.

21

How to Write News Stories: The Inverted Pyramid

——❖——

One of the staples of journalism is a story structure known as the "inverted pyramid." Why the name? Because the story starts at the tip of the pyramid and works its way toward the base.

Here's how it works:

1) You start with what happened.

2) Then you explain *why* it happened.

3) Last, you add commentary and other interesting, but not necessarily essential, background.

Here's the story of the three little pigs, told in inverted pyramid style:

> "A wooden home in Pleasantville was reduced to matchsticks last night when a long-standing feud between a wolf and a family of bachelor pigs erupted into violence. A police spokesperson said feuds of this kind are 'predictable

occurrences between natural enemies.' A neighbor said, 'I warned those pigs to build with brick.'"

■ Get to the point ... fast

The inverted pyramid is an editorial convenience. If space is tight, a news editor can simply trim paragraphs off the bottom of the story, safe in knowing that the really important information is at the top. Hence the first sentence of the above pigs story.

But that's probably not why you want the inverted pyramid in your bag of tricks. You'll want it handy because you're painfully aware that almost no one reads past the first paragraph. The point of your story ("See what we've accomplished with your gift!") must be right up front – or there's a very real risk readers will miss it.

Do NOT slowly reveal your surprises. Your good news isn't a gift to be unwrapped. Putting key points in the second, third or subsequent paragraphs will merely cause many donors to miss those points completely.

When the leader of an outside accreditation team concludes that yours is "the best daycare center I've ever seen," don't hide that incredible accomplishment at the *end* of 250 other words (as one newsletter did). SHOUT IT!!! LOUD!!! IMMEDIATELY!!!

22

How to Write News Stories: Start with an Anecdote

——❖——

At least half of the front-page features in *The Wall Street Journal* start with a quick anecdote. Here are a few examples:

• "Elizabeth Grubesich was cooking in her bright yellow and white kitchen in August 2002, when she got a call from her doctor. He told her the cancer drug she believed was keeping her alive would no longer be available." (The article explains how a change in marketing strategy at a large pharmaceutical company can have fatal consequences.)

• "SAVANNAH RIVER SITE, S.C. – Eight years ago, scientists using a metal rod here to probe the radioactive depths of a nuclear-waste tank saw something that shocked them: a slimy, transparent substance growing on the end of the rod." (The goop scoop? "Extremophiles," microbes that survive in super-hostile environments.)

• "In late May 1997, a white Gulfstream IV jet with a blue stripe along its side touched down at a small airfield outside Seattle. (We're watching the first few frames of huge bribery scandal start to unfold.)

Why do anecdotes work so well to launch a story? I can think of a few good reasons:

• Anecdotes speak to our Inner Amiable. We like to meet new people and see how they behave in a situation. Anecdotes are intimate, too: we're right at the person's shoulder.

• Anecdotes speak to our Inner Expressive. A good anecdote dumps us into the middle of the action, at a pivotal moment in the drama.

• Anecdotes are fast and efficient. They require no translation. We understand what's going on instantly because it's all show, no tell. We watch one person or a few people do something. And in the process, we learn a lot just by observing.

Take a second look at *The Wall Street Journal* anecdotes. Note the use of concrete details to paint a picture in your mind: "cooking in her bright yellow and white kitchen," "metal rod," "a slimy, transparent substance," "a white Gulfstream IV jet with a blue stripe along its side." These details don't necessarily have news value. They don't always contribute important facts. But they do set the scene, so you can easily imagine it.

■ What makes a successful anecdote

A good anecdote has some or all of the following characteristics:

• It is rich in concrete detail. At a minimum a specific time, place, and problem. Remember: details are reassuring to the reader. They ("...a warm white bed in an apple green room that still smelled of fresh paint in the corners...") make an anecdote easy for the reader to visualize and understand. It's a form of "You are there!"

• It focuses on a single person or a couple. This kind of intense and intimate human interest warms up the reader's Inner Amiable.

• It shows either accomplishment or need. The donor is especially interested in those two things, as well as whether charity mattered.

• It has some emotion lurking beneath the surface (fear, anger, hope, relief, joy...)

• It is surprising, shocking: "Tell me something I don't know," begs the reader's Inner Expressive.

An anecdote can be fast. A mere flash. Brief is fine. You're not writing a novel or even a short story. Squirts of anecdotal information are enough.

When the donor newsletter from an adult literacy agency, for instance, mentions that Eddie Tomasso "finally admitted to his wife that he couldn't read when he was 56 years old," that one small but dazzling anecdotal detail is all the proof I need (combined with the knowledge that Eddie now reads just fine) to know that this organization helps people in profound ways.

23

Fatal Flaw No. 4: Hogging the Credit

———❖———

An effective donor newsletter will say the following, in some fashion, every chance it can: "With your help, we accomplished worthwhile things. And with your further generous support, we can do even more. But without your help, we won't accomplish nearly as much."

When you make your donors into heroes, you will raise more money. Treat them like the superheroes they are. They've invested in your dream. They've trusted you with a precious resource, their money. They believe in your mission. Here's the recurring theme: *With you, we can change the world. But not without you.*

The corollary: Don't hog the credit for your organization's good works. Share the credit with your donors. That's what they crave.

■ Donor recognition: The true meaning of

What is good donor recognition? Is it the brass plaque engraved with a donor's name? Is it a name in an annual report, listing the donor with dozens of others who have made gifts to your organization? Is it a hand-signed thank you note from the executive director?

All of the above. And none of the above.

Recognition is really about making the donor feel that his or her support matters deeply to your organization and the world, whether that support is $10 or $10,000.

Dale Carnegie, in his classic *How to Win Friends and Influence People* (first published in 1936 and still in print), has a lot to say about the basic human desire to feel important.

Carnegie lists eight things "every normal adult wants." These include health, food, sleep, money, sex, our children's well-being, "life in the hereafter." He adds, "But there is one longing almost as deep, almost as imperious, as the desire for food or sleep which is seldom gratified. It is what Freud calls 'the desire to be great.' It is what [American philosopher John] Dewey calls the 'desire to be important.'"

Bottom line: we want our lives to matter.

Beth Stafford, executive director of Manchester Area Conference of Churches, often asks her donors, "Do you have any idea of how important you are to the work we do?" When she reports her agency's accomplishments, the donor is placed front and center: "Could we provide over 40,000 meals a year to a hungry community in one year? NOT WITHOUT YOU we couldn't." Over and over she repeats this mantra.

A donor newsletter is *not* about what your agency has achieved. It's about what your donors have achieved *through* your agency. Tell your donors how important they are; that's the recognition they really want. Give them a share in the credit; don't take all the credit yourself.

Show your donors that you couldn't possibly accomplish your work without them. If you do that, they will return the compliment and support you generously for a good long time.

24

Fatal Flaw No. 5: Expecting People to Read Deep

———❖———

Watch yourself next time you pick up the newspaper.

You browse first. If you find something of interest, you start reading. And even then, often you read no more than a paragraph or two before you jump to another story, unless you're enjoying a leisurely morning.

It's the same for donors. When your newsletter arrives, the first thing they do is browse: skim a few headlines, look at the photos, maybe read a caption, to see if anything's of interest. If nothing is, they put the newsletter aside, likely never to return.

Which means, if you have nothing of interest in your "browser level" (*see the next chapter*), you've wasted your time and money.

Don't expect donors to read deep, because most of them won't. Assume 80 percent of your audience will read just the headline of any particular story (it's an assumption newspaper editors make).

25

The Browser Level

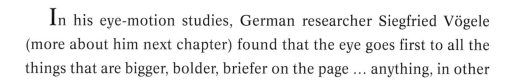

In his eye-motion studies, German researcher Siegfried Vögele (more about him next chapter) found that the eye goes first to all the things that are bigger, bolder, briefer on the page ... anything, in other words, that isn't dense, gray text.

Graphic designers sometimes call these "entry points": visual hot spots that attract the eye and invite the reader into a story.

■ The browser level: An inventory

A newsletter's browser level can have any or all of the following:

- Photos
- Illustrations
- Charts and graphs
- Headlines
- Subheads

- Lead paragraphs (especially if the paragraph is a single short sentence)
- Pull quotes
- Captions
- Bullet lists

Keep in mind: most information transfers at the browser level … or not at all. The browser level is also where you hook the interest of that small number of donors who will read deeper.

26

The Bouncing Eye

Siegfried Vögele electrified the direct marketing industry when he introduced his pioneering eye-motion research in the 1980s. This professor in Munich, Germany, rigged cameras to record how a reader's eyes jumped around when confronting an unfamiliar page of graphics and print.

It turned out that the eye was not only round like a ball. It bounced like one, too.

His findings have had an incalculable influence on the practice of direct marketing. It's fair to say that the scientific understanding of how we read divides into two periods, BV and AV: before Vögele and after. (And yet very few communicators outside direct marketing know of him. Ask your graphic designer if the name Siegfried Vögele rings a bell.)

In a quick search of the Internet you'll find numerous articles about Professor Vögele's research. But for our purposes, I'll mention a few of his key findings.

Encountering an open newsletter or magazine, he discovered, the eye typically enters at the upper righthand corner and moves immediately (and involuntarily) to the largest graphic on the page. The eye concludes its scan by exiting at the lower righthand corner.

That's the big picture. Vögele also found that eyes go to:

- Photographs or drawings first, before they go to text.
- Close-ups first, before they go to photos showing the entire person.
- Children first, before they go to adults.
- Big text (i.e., headlines) first, before they go to small text.
- Short words, short lines, and short paragraphs first (i.e., headlines, captions, pull quotes).

The implications? Well, for one thing you have far more control over what the viewer looks at than you might have realized. By deft use of bolder, bigger graphic elements (see the list in the preceding chapter), you can drag the reader's eye around almost at will.

27

Eliminate Gratuitous Visual Labor

❖

It's hard enough to get someone to read your articles (most people are reading just the headlines, remember). Don't make it even harder by adding visual labor: you *will* pay a price. The more visual labor you add, the more readers you lose.

There are four ways newsletters typically add visual labor to the experience of reading articles on a printed page:

1) By printing the articles in colored type

2) By printing the articles over colored backgrounds or on non-white paper

3) By printing the articles in reverse type (i.e., white type on a black or dark background)

4) By printing the articles in sans serif type (Arial or Helvetica are the most common sans serif typefaces)

It's hard sometimes to convince graphic designers of these facts, so I've included a few bits of relevant data below.

■ Wheildon's science erases centuries of opinion

Colin Wheildon, a distinguished Australian magazine editor, began researching readability issues in the 1980s. Vancouver-based fundraiser Harvey McKinnon ran across Wheildon's data and passed it along to Berkeley-based fundraiser Mal Warwick, whose Strathmoor Press published it in book form in 1995. That particular edition is long since out of print. But a new edition, titled *Type & Layout: Are You Communicating or Just Making Pretty Shapes*, appeared in 2005, from Worsley Press.

It's worth noting that Wheildon's research has had very limited circulation. And it's safe to say that few graphic designers know of it; I've yet to meet one who does.

Implausibly enough, Wheildon's research seems to be the first pure-science investigation regarding readability since Gutenberg introduced the printing press to Europe in the 1430s. Before Wheildon ran his tests, readability had been a matter of "informed" opinion, accepted wisdom, and hearsay.

Wheildon did his research to help his advertisers design better ads, among other things. But many of his findings apply to any reading matter, including newsletters.

In the table that follows (reprinted with permission from Colin Wheildon), I've summarized some of his key findings. These are the ones I think you need to know about, to evaluate your newsletter's design.

Design Choice	How Easy is it to Comprehend?		
Article in black ink on white paper	Good: 70%	Fair: 19%	Poor: 11%
Article in black ink on pale blue paper	Good: 38%	Fair: 19%	Poor: 43%
Article in black ink on white paper	Good: 70%	Fair: 19%	Poor: 11%
Article in purple ink on white paper	Good: 51%	Fair: 13%	Poor: 36%
Article in black on white background	Good: 70%	Fair: 19%	Poor: 11%
Article in white on black background	Good: 0%	Fair: 12%	Poor: 88%
Article in serif type	Good: 67%	Fair: 19%	Poor: 14%
Article in sans serif type	Good: 12%	Fair: 23%	Poor: 65%
Headlines in black	Good: 67%	Fair: 19%	Poor: 14%
Headlines in bright colors	Good: 17%	Fair: 18%	Poor: 65%
Headlines in dark colors	Good: 52%	Fair: 28%	Poor: 20%

■ Why reading sans serif type is slow as molasses

Colin Wheildon's research found that text set in sans serif type such as ...

Helvetica, Arial, and Avant Garde

is five times harder to comprehend than text set in serif type such as ...

Times New Roman, Garamond, or Palatino.

Why? In North America, anyway, most of the time you read serif typefaces, not sans serif. Most newspapers, magazines, and books are set in serif type. Serif type is the default. (You can easily confirm this for yourself next time you visit a bookstore. Glance at a dozen books chosen at random. You'll see that most are typeset in a serif font.) Your brain becomes accustomed to interpreting serif type at light speed.

Sans serif type, on the other hand, is relatively uncommon. Your brain finds these less familiar letters harder to process quickly. Recognition slows down, and so does reading.

Bear in mind, this all has to do with the *printed* page. Websites are different. There, sans serif faces are probably more common than serif faces. There's a reason: a computer screen has poor resolution compared to a printed page. A monitor does not display the fine strokes of serif type particularly well. Serif text at small sizes (12 point and below), which looks easy to read on the printed page, looks a bit blurred on a computer screen, where sans serif type still looks sharp.

28

Pull Quotes Bring Your Buried Treasures to Light

❖

Even if you're not familiar with the term "pull quote," you're very familiar with pull quotes themselves. You read them all the time, in newspapers and magazines. Pull quotes are an important reader convenience. As a reader, you use pull quotes all the time to decide at a glance whether or not you're interested in a story.

What is a pull quote (a.k.a. drop out quote, pullout quote, breakout or blurb)?

Dr. Barbara G. Ellis, author of *The Copy-Editing and Headline Handbook*, defines it thus: "A key quote from a story that has been lifted and [often] set in 14- to 18-point type with rules or boxes. It is used to break up the grayness of text, as well as to attract readers into the story."

Let's look at a brilliant example of that second use.

It appeared in a long profile of a technology firm. The profile ran in a national business magazine trusted by investors. Here's the pull quote the editors chose:

"There's no way they'll become profitable,"
says one analyst. "I don't think they'll survive."

Imagine the scene. An investor, idly flipping the pages, quickly spots that pull quote. It is, after all, the only bigger, easy-to-read type on a page otherwise filled with dense gray text. And it warns, in no uncertain terms: *Red alert! Company in trouble!*

Instantly, the former idle flipper changes into an avid reader, to sniff out the name of this potential loser before it costs her money.

That's the power of a well-chosen pull quote. If it hooks your interest, it stops you cold.

■ Pull quotes to the rescue

A pull quote can single-handedly rescue *your* message from oblivion.

I'm looking at a page from a rape crisis center newsletter. It is carpeted wall-to-wall with an article, a carefully researched article that someone labored over. It says important things about the bizarre twists of domestic violence. But the article has three strikes against it:

1) It has a misleading (vague, meek, tossed-off) headline: "Some Challenges We Face." A headline like that could be about almost anything from aardvarks to zealots.

2) It starts sluggishly, beginning with a history lesson (yawn). "The anti-rape movement as documented in traditional histories and timelines is by all accounts less than thirty years old."

3) It is dense, *visually* dense, with paragraphs and sentences that run on for miles.

Yet ... in this almost impenetrable article the author buries one amazing anecdote, an anecdote so shocking, so sickening it cries out for redress. If any donor ever read it.

But almost no one did. Why? Because that anecdote was buried 300 words deep, where virtually no one ever goes. I doubt five out of a thousand donors who received this newsletter ever read beyond the article's lecturing first words.

Which means they missed this red-hot poker:

> ...[our hotline] received a call from a woman who had not eaten anything but some slices of bread for days. Confined to a wheelchair, this woman [a paraplegic who could not unlock her chair] was starved by her husband, who would put food just out of her reach.

That brief but shocking anecdote is exactly the kind of story that brings the blood of true believers to a boil. And money flows from people on boil, if you ask them while they're hot. They're angry. They want to do something about this vile injustice right now. And your organization offers hope.

A pull quote would have saved that anecdote from oblivion. Repeating that anecdote as a pull quote, in big, bold type, would have brought it to the attention of countless more donors...and put its emotional treasure to work, inspiring your base with righteous anger.

Don't bury your best stuff. EXALT IT!!! ... in pull quotes.

29

Use Subheads to Break Up Columns of Dense Text

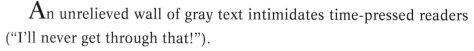

An unrelieved wall of gray text intimidates time-pressed readers ("I'll never get through that!").

If an article in your newsletter is more than a few paragraphs long, consider subheads (see facing page).

◼ Subheads break the monotony

Subheads perform many services.

They break a long story into easy digestible chunks.

They help structure the story by shining a spotlight on one key point in each subsection. They help the story unfold.

They act as stepping stones, allowing the reader to skip through the entire story briefly before digging in.

They can add momentum by revealing intriguing tidbits that advance the story.

Subheads Increase Readability

Affordable Housing 101: RI's crisis in a nutshell

Home prices soar. Incomes don't

Since 1999, rents and house prices have skyrocketed in Rhode Island. In six years the median sale price for a single-family home more than doubled. A home that someone purchased in 1999 for a median $126,000 turned around and sold in 2004 for $264,700.

At the same time, median household income in the state inched up a mere one percent annually, according to the U.S. Census.

A new reality for many

All Rhode Islanders can afford less and less house every year. Moderate-to-minimum wage earners in Rhode Island (the majority of our workforce) get it worst. Tens of thousands now face a new reality: you can hold down a steady job…yet be unable to afford to move up into a decent home and a better life.

Tens of thousands of Rhode Island's moderate-to-minimum wage earners have almost no choice but to live in substandard housing or go homeless. That's all they can find and afford in a galloping market with double-digit annual house appreciation.

Too few decent homes, too much demand

Many factors have contributed to the state's hyperactive real estate appreciation, says the RI Association of Realtors: "low interest rates…an uncertain stock market, quality of life, commutability, and buyers coming from other more expensive markets in bordering states."

Affordable Housing 101: RI's crisis in a nutshell

Since 1999, rents and house prices have skyrocketed in Rhode Island. In six years the median sale price for a single-family home more than doubled. A home that someone purchased in 1999 for a median $126,000 turned around and sold in 2004 for $264,700.

At the same time, median household income in the state inched up a mere one percent annually, according to the U.S. Census.

All Rhode Islanders can afford less and less house every year. Moderate-to-minimum wage earners in Rhode Island (the majority of our workforce) get it worst. Tens of thousands now face a new reality: you can hold down a steady job…yet be unable to afford to move up into a decent home and a better life.

Tens of thousands of Rhode Island's moderate-to-minimum wage earners have almost no choice but to live in substandard housing or go homeless. That's all they can find and afford in a galloping market with double-digit annual house appreciation.

Many factors have contributed to the state's hyperactive real estate appreciation, says the RI Association of Realtors: "low interest rates…an uncertain stock market, quality of life, commutability, and buyerscoming from other more expensive markets in bordering states."

The biggest factor, though, is a basic economics: supply and demand. "Strong demand relative to supply has contributed to significant increases in the median price," the Association noted in its 2003 report. Translation: we have too few decent homes in Rhode Island with too much money chasing them. Net result: house prices go

The biggest factor, though, is a basic economics: supply and demand. "Strong demand relative to supply has contributed to significant increases in the median price," the Association noted in its 2003 report. Translation: we have too few decent homes in Rhode Island with too much money chasing them. Net result: house prices go ballistic.

House construction stuck in slow gear

Build your way out of a housing crisis, experts recommend. Having more units for sale cools an overheated market. But that's the other part of the problem: Rhode Island's housing production has fallen dramatically.

In 1986, a peak year, developers built 7,274 privately-owned units (houses and condominiums) in Rhode Island. In 2004, building of privately-owned units had fallen to just 2,532 units, according to the U.S. Census. Rhode Island's per capita construction rate is already among the very lowest in America, and shows no sign of improving . On the contrary: the number of new single-family units built in 2004 (1,903) was the smallest in two decades.

ballistic.

Build your way out of a housing crisis, experts recommend. Having more units for sale cools an overheated market. But that's the other part of the problem: Rhode Island's housing production has fallen dramatically.

In 1986, a peak year, developers built 7,274 privately-owned units (houses and condominiums) in Rhode Island. In 2004, building of privately-owned units had fallen to just 2,532 units, according to the U.S. Census. Rhode Island's per capita construction rate is already among the very lowest in America, and shows no sign of improving . On the contrary: the number of new single-family units built in 2004 (1,903) was the smallest in two decades.

30

The AP Formula for Captions

———❖———

A caption is the "text describing a photograph or illustration," says Desktop Publishing by Design. Simple. Here's a formula for the standard two-sentence caption, from *The Associated Press Stylebook and Libel Manual*:

- The first sentence...describes what the photo shows, in the present tense, and states where and when the photo was made.

- The second sentence...gives background on the news event or describes why the [subject of the] photo is significant.

That second sentence is where you slip in your message, by providing a context for the events or people or objects shown.

(See photo on next page.)

A steady job but no affordable home: a man finds shelter with us while he hunts for his next apartment. Thanks to skyrocketing property values, 80 percent of the homeless we see have work but no place they can afford to rent.

Used with permission of the Manchester Area Conference of Churches

31

Your Column Width
Can Slow or Speed Reading

——❖——

People from time to time ask whether there's a perfect layout for a newsletter. I don't think so. Three-column is the stodgy default. The layout just doesn't matter that much if all your other "t's" are crossed and "i's" are dotted.

What does matter is column width. The perfect column width, the most reader-friendly column width, is between 40 and 60 characters wide, according to the experts.

Newspapers and news magazines have this down cold. They are designed to be read in minutes, not hours. I am looking at an issue of Newsweek. Its stories are set in columns that are 40 characters wide, in a serif typeface.

Desktop publishing has put at our fingertips power once wielded only by a priesthood of well-apprenticed graphic designers. Unfortunately, this democraticized power comes without knowledge of the principles of good design, so accidents happen. An example: donor newsletters with columns as wide as 110 characters.

The eye despairs.

Keep this in mind: your eye gets lost very easily on a printed page. Column widths exceeding 70 characters exacerbate this problem. Narrower columns help keep the problem in check.

32

Lower the Grade Level of Your Writing

———❖———

In my workshop, I ask students to read a long, academic passage that defines two literary terms: *metonymy* and *synecdoche*. Then I ask, "Guess what grade level those definitions were written at." The consensus opinion usually pegs the passage around the 12th-grade level or higher.

In fact, using the standard Flesch-Kincaid scale, the definitions score at the 8th-grade level. My point is this: you can write about anything, even astrophysics, at the 8th-grade level.

And you should.

Newspapers write near the 8th-grade level. They're not trying to write down to their readers. They are trying to make their information fast and easy to absorb. On slow days, I will check a few paragraphs from a *Wall Street Journal* feature article, just to see. Most score in the 8th- to 10th-grade range.

Direct mail, which puts a high premium on speed, is written at a low grade level. One of my most successful direct mail campaigns added more than 500 millionaires to a community foundation's hot prospect list. That letter, which became a national model, scores around the 6th-grade level.

That is not to brag, you understand. It's to point out that millionaires didn't feel patronized by the grade level. If they noticed anything about the writing at all, it was just how quickly they sped through the letter.

One more example. That detective novel you bought for your airplane flight? There's a good chance it's written at the 4th-grade level. Why? Because the lower the grade level, the faster the read. That's what makes a "page-turner" turn.

The preceding paragraphs, incidentally, score at the 6th-grade level.

■ It's all about those ratios

The most common objection I hear, when I tell people they should write at the 8th-grade level, is this: "All my readers are college educated. They don't need the material dumbed down."

People often misunderstand the grade-level issue. It's not a question of "dumbing down." It's a question of speeding up.

Readers want to get through your stuff as fast as possible. They have busy lives. Write much above the 8th-grade level, and you'll slow them down. Ease of comprehension and grade level are directly linked. Raise your grade level and ease of comprehension slows. Lower your grade level and ease of comprehension speeds up.

It doesn't matter what vocabulary you use, by the way. Really. Feel free to use scientific terms, medical terms, economic terms, whatever suits you.

What *does* matter in your writing will be the ratios: the ratio of short words to long, the ratio of short sentences to long, the ratio of short paragraphs to long. You want to strongly favor the short over the long whenever possible. The higher your ratio of short to long, the lower your grade level.

In this context, 'and' is a dangerous word. People will often take two perfectly fine short sentences and join them with an *and*, making a longer, gangly, harder to absorb sentence. Don't use *and* without good reason.

The preceding section scores at just below the 6th-grade level.

■ How to score your grade level

I'm loath to recommend Microsoft Word. I consider it an elephant pretending to be a tap dancer. But one of Word's virtues is its built-in grammar checker. The grammar checker allows you to score the grade level of your prose.

When I write anything for a client, I score my grade level obsessively, sometimes every few minutes. I consider it unacceptable to turn in text written above the 8th-grade level. People hire me to please readers, not to make them work.

In my version of Word (for the Mac), the grammar checker is found in the Tools menu, under Spelling and Grammar. If this feature isn't working in your Word, it's probably not turned on. Go to your Preferences and make sure you've selected both "Check grammar with spelling" and "Show readability statistics."

The preceding section scores at just above the 7th-grade level.

33

Fatal Flaw No. 6:
Non- or Feeble Headlines

First the bad news: The vast majority of donor newsletters I've seen (sent to me for analysis by hundreds of organizations) have either weak headlines or no real headlines at all.

Now let me explain *why* this is bad news. I'll pose a question first: Which is more important: The headline? Or the article?

You might reasonably assume the article is the real star. It took ages to research and write. It's packed with information. It's long.

But not so fast. Think about it: no one reads an article who wasn't first lured in by a headline. Here's the kicker: experts say that very few people ever read past the headlines. *Four out of five readers stop right there*, it's assumed. In our time-pressed, over-informed world, people prefer to grab-and-go. A headline's plenty, thank you.

So the correct answer is: in terms of numbers of readers reached, headlines matter more – far, *far* more – than the stories that follow them. Only a tiny minority of your donors will ever read beyond the headline, and maybe the first couple of paragraphs, of any story.

Your messages *must* penetrate via your headlines, if they are going to penetrate at all. You *must* write effective headlines, or your newsletter is a waste of time and money.

■ The true purpose of headlines

Headlines aren't just the bigger type at the top of the article. Headlines have a demanding job. That job is to summarize the story, so readers can decide whether they want to read any deeper.

"Well-written headlines are the main entry point to text," notes Dr. Mario R. Garcia, in his book, *Redesigning Print for the Web*. He is an international authority on newspaper design. "A good headline [has] enticing words, good action verbs, the best possible summary of what the content is about, and, if possible, a surprise or 'hook' that pulls us in."

In the special case of donor newsletters, the headline has *two* jobs:

1) To summarize the story; and

2) To do so in a way that reveals accomplishment, need, mission or vision – all the things that donors respond to.

■ Warning: These are not real headlines

Here's a sampling of front-page "headlines" ripped from donor newsletters in my files (and I wasn't trying to be mean):

- Strategic Plan on the Move
- Willis Center & Diversity R-E-S-P-E-C-T
- East Side Initiates NRZ
- An Inclusive Approach to Excellence
- Leadership Institute
- The Value of Volunteering
- Adoption Works!

• A Message from Jim Franklin, Gift Planning Counselor

I want you to read that list again. Only this time think like a donor and ask yourself: "Do I still have questions regarding what each story is about? Do I still wonder why the story matters?"

Of course you do. You still have questions because these are not real headlines. They failed to do at least three things that any professionally written headline would do:

1) Clearly explain the gist of the story.

2) Reveal to the target audience why the story matters.

3) Have a hook (something new, different, intriguing).

You've just learned an important skill: how to spot a dysfunctional headline in your own newsletter. It's easy. Read the headline as if you'd never seen it before (maybe read it to a friend, if you need a really objective opinion). The headline alone should tell you (or your friend) what the story is about and why it matters to a donor. If not, your headline needs a rewrite.

■ Time management

If you now spend hours writing your articles and a few minutes writing your headlines, reverse that habit. Instead, spend hours writing your headlines and minutes writing your articles.

I'm exaggerating, but you get my point. Don't toss off your headlines. They're far too important. You need to write them as if the story itself didn't exist, and all your eggs were in your headline basket.

34

Case Study: Hospital Headline Aims, Misses

It was a feature story in the hospital's donor newsletter. Headline:

**Legislators Don White Coats
to Examine Medical Education Funding**

Tucked in one corner was a snapshot of politicians wearing lab coats. The photographer had just said, "Smile!" obviously. Everyone was beaming.

To judge from the headline (abetted by the photo), you might conclude that the story was about "Pols play doctor dress-up."

But no. The real story was this: cuts in federal funding have caused a fall-off in medical school enrollments. Lacking sufficient federal funds, medical schools (and this hospital is affiliated with one) are graduating too few new doctors.

Bad news, readers: there are no longer enough physicians to keep pace. Patient volume is already expanding three to five percent a year. It will soon rise, roaring like a moon rocket, when Baby Boomers reach their retirement years. And there won't be enough doctors to go around.

But none of that's mentioned in the headline. Or in the article either, for that matter. I had to dig it out of the writer.

■ When you write your headline, remember your audience

The point I want to make with this case study: when you write headlines, bear in mind the emotional interests of your audience.

The average age of a hospital donor is probably 60 (at least). As people get on in years, they begin to worry more and more about their health and its failings. After age 50, as my older sister Alice says, "it's all repair, repair, repair."

People are afraid of falling ill. Knowing this about your donors, a better headline for a story on federal funding would have added a dose of fear:

**Cuts in Federal Funding Slash Med School
Applications. Will You Have a Doctor
When You Need One?**

I imagine you're screaming (silently), "Are you kidding? You want me to scare old people?"

Well, feel free to do it with wit and grace, but yes: that is exactly what you have to do to overcome the natural-born inertia of your audience. If the goal in this story's case was to fire up donors to get on the phone and demand from their Congressional delegation an immediate increase in federal funding to medical schools, you will need to use an emotional trigger or two.

35

How to Write Great Headlines

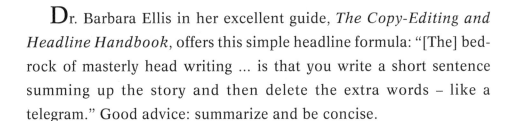

Dr. Barbara Ellis in her excellent guide, *The Copy-Editing and Headline Handbook*, offers this simple headline formula: "[The] bedrock of masterly head writing ... is that you write a short sentence summing up the story and then delete the extra words – like a telegram." Good advice: summarize and be concise.

But not too concise.

Unless you're reporting *Titanic Sinks*, it's unlikely your summary will pack down into just a couple of words.

I have on my desk the latest issue of *The Wall Street Journal*. There are four front-page feature stories. The average length of their headlines is 25 words, if you count the head, the kicker and the deck together.

■ "Kicker? Deck? Say what?"

You might be unfamiliar with the terms "kicker" and "deck." Let me show you what I'm referring to, with this example pulled from a donor newsletter:

Knock, knock. Who's there? Kids who want to study!

Up 177%: Demand Soars for Club's Free Afterschool Homework Program

Project Learn can turn "C" students into "B" students

The "knock, knock" line is the *kicker*. The kicker is a fragmentary bit of text above the headline. It's also called in the trade an eyebrow: it winks at you. Kickers flirt, tease, hint. It's typeset in a small point size.

The "Up 177%" line is the *headline*. It's typeset in a large point size.

The "Project Learn" line is the *deck*. That's the official journalistic term. Civilians would call it a subhead. It's typeset in a point size that's smaller than the headline but larger than the article. You can have more than one deck, incidentally. I've run stories with up to four decks.

Kickers are optional. Decks are indispensable.

Headlines and decks really work together as a single unit. One tells the tale. The other comments on the tale. Journalism guru Ann Wylie offers these guidelines:

- Use the headline to telegraph a single, newsworthy story in eight words or less.

- Add information in a deck of 14 words or less. Take a view. Do not repeat the same information as the headline.

- In the first sentence of your first paragraph (what editors call the *lead*) answer two questions: "What happened?" and "Why should the reader care?"

An observation: 99 out of 100 nonprofit newsletters I see do not use decks at all. That's a big wasted opportunity, because anyone who reads a headline will probably also read the deck. Few will read the article itself.

36

Case Study: Foundation Headline Looks Right, All Wrong

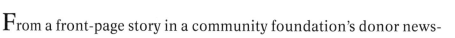

From a front-page story in a community foundation's donor newsletter:

(Head)

Family Literacy, Quality Childcare and Family Preventive Healthcare Top Priorities for Early Childhood Initiative

(Deck)

Alliance Brings Successful Literacy Program to Area

(Lead sentence)

In partnership with the Humanities Council, the Foundation is funding Motheread, Inc., to help this community strengthen the bond between parents and their children.

The front end looks right. There's a head, a deck, and a lead working together. So what's wrong?

1) *It is an indigestible lump of verbal gristle.*

Together, the head, deck and lead score at the 12th grade level. They earn a dismal reading-ease score of 15 out of a possible 100. At bottom, this opening is more of a barrier than a welcome mat.

Are the pros any different? I scored a *Wall Street Journal* front end (head, deck, lead) that came randomly to hand. The *Journal's* very digestible lump scored at the 6th grade level, with a reading ease score of 72 out of 100.

The pros know: if you want to hook browsers, you have to start with something that's a breeze to read.

Reading is no different than any other form of exercise. People hit your story cold. They're not ready for hard labor. They need to warm up. If your opening paragraph is a gruesome chore, they'll flee the scene.

2) *The headline treats jargon as if it were generally acceptable language.*

Jargon is shorthand, a convenience for a trade or profession. A social worker might understand in depth what is meant by terms like "family preventive healthcare" and "early childhood initiative." But the donor won't.

Avoid jargon when you're writing for a non-specialist audience. Jargon is private and exclusive. It says, in effect, "You're not one of us." Readers, as you might imagine, can find that offensive.

3) *From the donor's perspective, the lead does a poor job of answering Ann Wylie's two key questions: "What happened?" and "Why should I care?"*

Inconsequential information abounds: "In partnership with the

Humanities Council, the Foundation is funding Motheread, Inc. ...”
Donors first and foremost want to know how you're changing the community. The names of the players don't matter all that much.

What *does* matter is what you hope to accomplish with the new program, here described as an attempt to “strengthen the bond between parents and their children.” And who knows what that really means? Is bonding something the community desperately needs? Are mothers and their children unbonded now? The statement is vague.

Readers don't respond to vague. They respond to specifics, scenes they can see in their head. This story would have thrived had it led with an anecdote that shined a spotlight on the problem.

> “Jimmy is only four years old, but he's already an educational casualty, studies suggest. Why? Because his mother doesn't read to him. She can't. She's illiterate. A new program hopes to fix that problem for the city's poorest young mothers.”

37

Fatal Flaw No. 7: Stat Crazy, Anecdote Lite

———❖———

With every issue of your donor newsletter you advance your case for support. Two kinds of evidence help you with this task: statistical evidence and anecdotal evidence.

Both kinds are factual (since ethical organizations don't lie). But that doesn't mean they both work alike. Quite the contrary.

Statistical evidence (data) tends to speak to the intellect. (And it's never a mistake to treat your donors as intelligent human beings.) Anecdotal evidence, though, tends to speak directly to the heart. Anecdotes trigger the emotions fast. And as we learned in Chapters 14, stirred emotions lead to gifts.

To make your strongest case for support, you need both statistics and anecdotes. Yet many nonprofits rely almost exclusively on statistical evidence to convince people that their work is important. And that's a mistake. Environmental advocacy groups and other science-based organizations are especially prone to this error.

Statistics have their place, don't get me wrong. But they can be surprisingly weak persuaders when you're trying to move people to give.

38

Tips on Using Statistics Well

———❖———

Please forgive this weary cliché, but too often when we use statistics to persuade, we assume "size matters." We slap on the table our extremely large number and stand back proudly. The implication: "Isn't this amazing? Isn't this huge number, by itself, powerful, convincing, wonderful or a low-down dirty shame?"

■ The fickle nature of really big numbers

Keep in mind each reader judges your extremely large number against a context you cannot know or predict.

Two examples:

• A museum came to me very excited. They had had a record year: 75,000 tickets sold, their best attendance ever. As it happened, though, I had a similar client. My client attracted 750,000 annual paying visitors, ten times as many.

From my end of the telescope, the museum's record attendance seemed nice but not all that impressive. They thought they were doing a great job. I thought (quietly, to myself) that they could do a lot better.

• A large Midwestern environmental group published its annual report. In it, the editor prominently trumpeted this statistic: "Program staff logged more than 16,700 miles on the road assisting local groups across the state."

I live in Rhode Island, the smallest state in America. My wife, the consultant, easily logs 20,000 miles on the road each year, assisting her clients. I'm thinking, "You mean to say your entire staff, in a huge state, drives fewer miles than my wife, in the tiniest state? You people have *got* to get out of the office more!"

You see the problem. What's the solution? Make sure you provide enough context to reveal your statistic's true meaning.

Never assume your readers will correctly read between the lines. Come right out and tell people what to think. "Program staff logged 16,700 miles on the road helping local groups across the state get their voices heard. Those local, and now quite vocal, groups made the winning difference this year in our battle against the state's worst corporate polluters!"

To repeat: your big, honking statistic by itself isn't important. What *is* important is what the statistic means.

■ How much of the problem did you solve?

The example below is an attempt by a very busy homeless shelter and soup kitchen to show its donors what the agency had accomplished in a year. I quote:

> Our Food Pantry welcomed 1,539 visits that received five days of groceries matching the needs of 664 different households; households comprised of 680 children, 843 adults and 38 seniors. Open mornings, five days per week, the pantry experienced an average of better than 6 visits per day.

Honestly: Can you tell from that untidy stack of numbers whether the agency succeeded or not? Can you tell whether the agency's programs fixed a tiny fraction of the problem or a very large piece? And can you tell if charity mattered at all? Those are among the key questions in donors' minds.

If you're summarizing your accomplishments, make sure you answer the following questions:

1) How much of the problem did you solve?
2) How much of the problem is left to solve?
3) How vital are donations to your solutions?

The Food Pantry could have told its story this way:

No one really knows how bad the hunger problem has become in our town.

What we *do* know is that this year we served 28 percent more free meals than last year.

What we *do* know is that this year we're seeing lots more families with kids in our meal lines: a 76 percent jump.

What we *do* know is that we have to raise *twice* as much money this year, so our cupboards won't run bare.

The Food Pantry is the only way many parents and seniors can still make ends meet, as rents and utility bills continue their double-digit annual rise.

Your help is critical to the town's hungriest. Can you double your gift this year?

■ Make one point per stat

Years ago I took a course on charts and graphs taught by a scientist. Here's a piece of his best advice:

Think of each statistic as a spear: it should have just one point.

Too often with statistics, we assume more is more, and pile them on, hoping I suppose we'll convince people by the sheer mass of our evidence. Fine, if researchers are your target audience. But donors are looking for meaning. And they want it fast. Make sure you pick statistics that tell a story, clearly and concisely.

Here's a great example, from a brochure distributed by the Edmonton (Alberta) SPCA

The headline advises:

End Her Cattin' Around

The subhead says:

They can't read or write ... but they sure can MULTIPLY!

Beneath that is a drawing of a pyramid of pets, and an explanation:

> One male and one female cat (and their offspring), when left to breed uncontrolled (assuming none are spayed or neutered), can produce more than 80,000 cats in 10 years!

Yikes! Stop the cat-alanche! Just tell me what to do! And the brochure does.

■ Include an emotional trigger

A single well-chosen stat can burn like a road flare to illuminate a problem and cast it into sharp relief ... *especially* when the stat has emotional resonance for the donor.

Here's an example, from a case statement used in a campaign to raise $5 million (successfully) for Hospice of the Chesapeake:

> Anne Arundel and Prince George's counties are about to get much older. In the next decade, the 65+ population will explode, increasing by 25 percent, with no end in sight. Hospice urgently needs to add capacity.

The emotional trigger here, in case you missed it, is fear. Fear is Old Reliable, the emotion voted "most likely to get people to act." As I've said before, when you're writing for donors, the correct sequence is "heart first and the head will follow."

39

Anecdotes vs. Stats

Anecdotes have certain advantages over statistics when you're talking to donors and other laypeople. Consider.

Statistics are:

- Sometimes hard to understand without "translation."
- Abstract by nature (they're numbers after all). Which makes them difficult to picture in your mind.
- Exclusive: just a few people such as program pros and other specialists understand the real implications.
- Neutral (i.e., scientific and objective).

Anecdotes, on the other hand, are:

- Understood instantly: no translation necessary.
- Concrete and specific. You can easily imagine them. They unfold like scenes.

- Inclusive: readily understood by anyone.
- Often dramatic (i.e., passionate and committed).

Here's my favorite example of an effective anecdote. A Boston charter school uses this tiny tale to prove just how quickly their innovative teaching methods can reverse a failing school career:

> When the pupil entered our third grade, she couldn't spell "cat." At the end of the year, she could spell "Tchaikovsky."

Consider the power compressed into that anecdotal sliver. I'm immediately impressed, of course: I had to look up how to spell *Tchaikovsky*. I also know that researchers have found that if a child isn't reading well by third grade, she's very likely to struggle forever.

Which means, in just 21 words I am utterly convinced that this school does amazing work ... and has saved a life.

40

How Often Should We Mail? Scheduling and Frequency

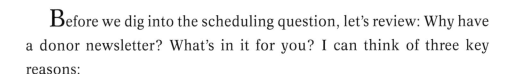

Before we dig into the scheduling question, let's review: Why have a donor newsletter? What's in it for you? I can think of three key reasons:

- It's a way to stay in touch with all your donors and let them know what you've accomplished with their money. A good donor newsletter breeds loyalty.

- It's a cultivation tool: it helps you prepare donors to be asked for more and bigger gifts (including bequests and other planned gifts).

- It's a source of income itself (assuming you make a good case and include a gift envelope).

Considering all that, how often should you mail? The Domain

Group, probably the world's foremost authority on donor newsletters, advises, "As often as possible."

What does that really mean? As often as you can manage to get something worth reading out the door. In some organizations, that will be twice a year. In a few organizations, that will be every month.

Pastor John at Community Emergency Service mails monthly. Often he'll send nothing more than a single sheet of paper printed both sides, mailed in an envelope with a reply envelope enclosed. His newsletter is the rough equivalent of a collection plate circulated by mail among the faithful (those who care about his mission).

■ My big, fat, infrequent newsletter

A bad trade-off is the big, fat newsletter that takes months to develop and burdens the staff. Newsletters don't have to be magazine length. It is better to get something brief out six times a year than to get something long out once a year. Why? Something called the Rule of Seven.

According to marketing consultant, Dr. Jeffrey Lant, the Rule of Seven says you need to be in touch with your prospect seven times in an 18-month period to guarantee a sale. Essentially, the Rule of Seven deals with the problem of inertia. People don't act immediately. They have to be reminded quite often.

It's the same in fundraising. Every time you remind "the predisposed" (the people who really care) of your mission, vision, urgency and need, more will respond. With each reminder, you overcome more inertia in your target audience. Some of those reminders come in the form of newsletters, some come in the form of direct mail solicitations, some might come in the form of emails or event invitations.

Can you mail too often? Yes and no. Yes, if you send out a fatally flawed newsletter. No, if your newsletter's worth reading.

41

An Easy Alternative: The Newsy-letter

Instead of always going to the time and expense of designing and printing an official-looking newsletter, try fleshing out your schedule with a less formal hybrid, the so-called "newsy-letter."

The newsy-letter is the equivalent of a letter to mom. It's a chatty update. News-filled. Unstuffy. Anywhere from two to four pages long. It's not a business letter. It's not a solicitation letter (though feel free to enclose a gift envelope). It's more like a phone conversation in print. "Hey, I'm just calling to let you know about some stuff that's happening...."

Here's the opening from a real-life example:

Dear Jane Donor,

I'm writing today to bring you up to date on a year's worth of amazing, wonderful, promising – and even scary things – that have happened at the Boys & Girls Club of Pawtucket.

First of all ... let me say thank you.

This year, your gift was especially important....

The newsy-letter offers you a fast way to get something out the door to donors. Bang it out. Don't overthink it. You're just saying hi. Talk about the organization's best accomplishments in the last few months. Talk about pressing needs or aspirations. Copiously thank the donor for his or her past contributions to your mission and vision. Sign your name. You're done.

You might be tempted to turn your newsy-letter into a solicitation letter. It's fine to make a small ask. But the point of the newsy-letter is to bear news, not to push for gifts.

42

E-Newsletters

In her 2003 book, *Donor-Centered Fundraising*, Penelope Burk reported, "Over 90 percent of individual donors in [our] study use email as a form of communication and 47 percent said they would appreciate receiving charities' newsletters and other information electronically."

By now probably 98 percent of individual donors use email to communicate. Whether 47 percent still want to receive electronic information from their charities I don't know. The war against spam has killed many innocent bystanders.

But let's be optimistic. Let's assume your donors love you so much they're happy to have you visit their email in-boxes.

■ The advantages of e-newsletters

E-newsletters have several advantages over paper newsletters.

• E-newsletters eliminate two major costs, printing and postage.

An e-newsletter prepared without benefit of a designer and sent from your own computers could end up costing you nothing but your time.

• E-newsletters are usually brief (and they should be). Since there's less to write, it's easier to crank out an issue. Which means you could also find it easier to stay in touch with your donor base more frequently (a good thing). Pithy, weekly updates are not uncommon.

Green Door, a Washington, D.C. organization that prepares adults with mental illnesses to work and live independently, publishes a monthly Wish List that attracts good response. Items are personalized: "An umbrella and raincoat for Pearlie." "A collapsible grocery cart for Deborah who just moved into an apartment." "Clarence needs sturdy work pants (40 waist x 32 length)."

• E-newsletters can be almost instantaneous. If you're an advocacy organization with a white-hot issue or a charity with an urgent need, it's possible to have a call to action in the hands of your supporters in a matter of minutes.

• E-newsletters help drive people to your website on a regular basis. The Seattle Children's Theatre (SCT) is a good example. Each monthly issue of SCT's e-newsletter contains just a handful of brief teasers. These teasers are about 25 words in length and end with the word "more." Clicking on "more" jumps the reader to the full story on the SCT website.

The Rhode Island Foundation sends out just one 50-word story every week in its e-newsletter. Each story includes a live link that jumps the reader to a section of the Foundation's website. By reviewing visitor statistics (data on who views which web pages on which days), the Foundation has developed a much better understanding of people's true interests.

■ Paper or electrons?

Given these advantages, you might well wonder: Is an e-newsletter an effective substitute for a paper newsletter? Can I switch completely to electronic news?

Maybe. The Seattle Children's Theatre, for instance, found that it sold lots more tickets when it switched from a paper newsletter to an e-newsletter. The e-newsletter offered greater convenience: people could instantly purchase tickets online, 24 hours a day. But theirs is a marketing newsletter, not a donor newsletter.

People are still habituated to paper. And it has its own advantages. It's tactile. You can put it down and return to it. You can file it. Bear in mind, too, that the average age of donors to many nonprofits is 60 and older.

These people grew up reading newspapers, not text messages on their cell phones. Paper is a familiar and comforting part of their world. There could well be an all-electronic future ahead for donor communications, but I don't think we're there quite yet.

Furthermore, I think a paper newsletter can have higher perceived value than an email. I suspect that e-newsletters and other e-communications are *too* easy to ignore. Hit the "delete" button, and it's gone. I offer this proof. It's not about newsletters, but it does offer an insight into how people treat their email.

One of my nonprofit clients runs workshops. We promote these workshops using a combination of direct mail and email. And the workshops routinely fill. Recently, though, we experimented. We skipped the direct mail piece, relying exclusively on emailed announcements instead. We got a nasty surprise: almost no one signed up.

Results like that make me cautious about abandoning mailed paper communications.

■ It must be opt-in

One last word of advice from the experts. Don't just add people to your e-mailing list willy-nilly. Run what's called an "opt-in" program. The Internet is about choice. Ask donors if they want your e-newsletter; don't just throw it at them. Even if you already have their email addresses, ask your donors if they want to receive your e-newsletter. And also provide an easy way to opt-out. Run a statement such as the following at the very top of every issue:

> You have subscribed to this e-newsletter. If you wish to unsubscribe, simply reply with "unsubscribe" in the subject line.

43

How Should It Look?
Domain Group's Proven Formula

——❖——

A few years ago I heard an executive from the Domain Group (Seattle, Atlanta, London) speak at an international conference. His topic: using donor newsletters to raise money.

Working with hundreds of clients through the years, the Domain Group has learned exactly how to transform the donor-focused newsletter from a bit player into a star. Here's the kicker: some of their clients now raise more money through donor newsletters than they do through direct mail solicitation letters. That's impressive...and food for thought.

At the conference, the Domain Group recommended the following formula for raising money with your newsletter:

- 11x17 format, folding to four 8.5 x 11 pages, sometimes with an extra sheet slipped in if you need more room

- Two-color printing (I've used one-color printing - black ink on white paper) with good results; Domain now finds that full-color printing does just as well

- Not on glossy paper

- NOT a self-mailer (self-mailers have "low perceived value," Domain believes)

- Mail in a #10 envelope with teaser copy: "Your newsletter enclosed."

- Send exclusively to current donors

- Include a reply envelope and reply device

- Mail as often as possible

- Focus on "accomplishment reporting" (my default formula is one-third accomplishments, one-third need, one-third recognition)

I have tested the Domain Group's formula repeatedly. It works.

44

My Closing Pep Talk

———❖———

It's easy: a profitable donor newsletter.

You just have to share the credit for all your hard and successful work.

You just have to remember that reading is labor, and reduce the labor.

You just have to honor the emotional reasons why your donors came to you in the first place.

You just have to deliver the news. And answer the question with passion and proof, "What did you do with the money?"

Don't overthink it. It's far more important to get your newsletter out than to get it "perfect." Furthermore, you'll improve in every issue. Guaranteed. And improving slowly is normal.

My last tip: Start to write better headlines. Your headlines produce most of your revenue.

Lesson over.

APPENDIX

What a Successful Donor Newsletter Looks Like

For your poking and prodding pleasure: the next four pages show what a modest, though effective, donor newsletter looks like.

The Pawtucket Boys & Girls Club mails each issue in a #10 envelope that bears the legend:

Dear believer in the kids of Pawtucket...
Your newsletter is inside.

The circulation is tiny right now, because the individual donor program is fairly new. The Pawtucket Boys & Girls Club has about 400 donors and hot prospects on its mailing list. The Club mails several newsletters a year; not enough, but it's a start.

The Club encloses a gift envelope with the newsletter. And after each mailing at least $2,000 comes back in those gift envelopes. It takes about a day and a half to write and design each issue.

You'll notice that the front page story is about a challenge grant. That's because challenge grants typically spur donors to give more.

You'll also notice that the accomplishment reporting is linked directly to need. The subtext in every issue is the same: we're so successful with our programs for kids, that we're growing almost out of control, and we need a ton more money to cover the bill.

The Club learned early that when its front page focused on accomplishment and downplayed need, the newsletter raised less in gifts. When the front page focused on need that was caused by accomplishment, giving went back up.

Illustration 1 - Boys & Girls of Pawtucket News

Winter 2005

Boys & Girls Club of Pawtucket News

One Moeller Place, Pawtucket, RI 02860 • 401-722-8840 • www.bgcpawt.org

NOW is best time to give. Why? Your gift automatically **DOUBLES**!

Three new "challenge" grants could spur Club's 2005 fiscal comeback

- Within reach (with your help): $210,000 in cash for Pawtucket kids
- Philanthropic alum and his novelist wife put $50,000 on the line; their personal biggest
- Club's board president and Citizens Bank add to challenge

DONORS, START YOUR CHECKBOOKS... and DOUBLE your giving instantly. NEW challenge grants:

- **Anthony Ruddy and Lisa Baumgarten (husband and wife, both Club alums, in his case from Pawtucket; she's a best-selling novelist under the pen name Lisa Gardner):**
  $50,000 CHALLENGE

- **Pawtucket Club board president Philip A. Ayoub:**
  $30,000 CHALLENGE

- **Citizens Bank, led by President and CEO (and Pawtucket Club alum) Joseph J. MarcAurele:**
  $25,000 CHALLENGE

Are YOU ready to meet the challenge for Pawtucket's boys and girls? Call Nisia Hanson at 722-8840.

Club alums have pledged $105,000 in 2005 if other donors can be found to make matching gifts. The total take (challenge and full match) amounts to $210,000. At stake: the future of the Pawtucket Club.

Increasing the level of community support has become a top priority at the Boys & Girls Club of Pawtucket. After the schools, the Club is Pawtucket's busiest child development agency, with 3,050 children and teens now enrolled in programs.

But it has struggled to find enough funding to keep pace with surging growth and a red-hot demand for services.

The three challenge grants hope to spur current donors to increase their giving, by offering people who care about the mission of the Club a chance to double the impact of their gifts.

Job #1: replacing bygone funding

Most of the private philanthropy the Pawtucket Club could count on 20 and 30 years ago has disappeared along with the city's manufacturing base.

The competition for grant funding in Rhode Island has intensified as well. The number of IRS-registered charities here now exceeds 5,000, more than double what it was in 1990.

With all these mouths to feed, traditional sources of support like the United Way, which pools charitable gifts collected from workplaces throughout the state, have found less and less every year to give the Pawtucket Club. (Though 2005 will see a temporary reversal of fortune. The United Way has awarded the Club two separate 21-month grants, recognizing the unusual effectiveness of our afterschool and preschool programs.)

It's left to each community to support vital social services. Developing a broader base of individual and business support from the community it serves has become essential for the Boys & Girls Club's financial health.

Finding $1,000 per child per year

Every child costs the Club more than $1,000 annually. The Club provides a safe and supervised place after school; year-round

...CHALLENGE continues on back

Illustration 2 - Boys & Girls of Pawtucket News

Number of single-parent households soars in Pawtucket; many are poor

Pawtucket's percentage leap is biggest by far among Rhode Island's cities

- The new reality: majority of Club members live with single moms, often in low-wage jobs
- Child poverty linked to variety of risks including teen pregnancy and adult joblessness

Why kids need the help they get at the Boys & Girls Club, now more than ever . . .

1996
26% of Pawtucket's kids live in SINGLE-PARENT households

Now
42% of Pawtucket's kids live in SINGLE-PARENT households

The percentage of single-parent households grew faster in Pawtucket than in any other Rhode Island city, reports the 2004 Rhode Island Kids Count Factbook. Rhode Island Kids Count is the state's leading researcher of child development issues.

From 1996 to 2004, the number of single-parent households in Pawtucket jumped from 26% to 42%, a steep 62% increase. Second-place Woonsocket's total grew just 48% in the same period.

At least 65% of the Club's members, we estimate, now live in single-parent households, most often led by a mom.

As a group, single moms have the lowest median income in Rhode Island, $17,252 a year (the single dad median is $29,776; the married couple with kids median is $63,706).

Studies show that children from poor, single-parent households face numerous disadvantages.

They are at higher risk for health and behavioral problems. They experience difficulty more often in school, are more often teen parents, earn less as adults, and are more often unemployed as adults.

Grants received since last we spoke...

- **Alperin/Hirsch Family Foundation**...$500...for general programming
- **Billy Andrade-Brad Faxon Charities for Children**...$9,625...for food for teens and transportation to and from the Elson Branch for after-school programs *(Thanks to Board Member, Paul Keating!)*
- **Boys & Girls Club of America**...$2,000...for a photography program, IMAGE MAKERS

- **Bristol County Savings Charitable Foundation**... $10,000...for teen homework, food and career planning *(Thanks to Board Member, Mike Tamburro!)*
- **Carter Family Charitable Trust**...$5,000...for All Children's Theatre collaboration
- **June Rockwell Levy Foundation** ...$7,500... for arts for all ages
- **MacAdams Charitable Foundation**...$250... for general programming
- **Ocean State Charities**...$3,000...for teen arts program
- **RBC Dain Rauscher**...$2,000...for arts
- **Stop & Shop, Cottage Street, Pawtucket** ...$3,611...for general programming *(Thanks to the employees there!)*
- **United Way of Rhode Island**...$180,000 over 21 months...for after-school programs
- **United Way of Rhode Island**...$20,000 over 21 months...for the Growing and Learning Center: The Creative Curriculum

Pawtucket Club member Alvin Andrade

Photo by John C. Meyers

Illustration 3 - Boys & Girls of Pawtucket News

Trustee Representative Peter F. Kilmartin presents a House of Representatives Legislative Grant for $10,000 to Jim Hoyt, Club CEO. The grant helps pay for sports, fitness and recreation activities in the Club's after-school programs. Looking on, a brass relief of Club benefactor Robert Moeller.

New board members named

Newly elected to the board:

- William A. Cateli, Jr., state aid and finance specialist, Rhode Island Office of Municipal Affairs
- Augusto "Cookie" Rojas, Jr., assistant vice president and community development officer, Pawtucket Credit Union (and Club alum)
- Kathleen S. Sullivan, community relations, Collette Vacations

Inducted as 2005 trustees:

- Richard J. Blockson, general manager of The Times
- J. Jeffrey Calista, owner and president of LJC Sales, Inc., Pawtucket
- Robert Lee Williams, family service coordinator, Pawtucket Housing Authority (and Club alum)

53 East Avenue closes

Opened in 1902, building became too costly to maintain and update; teen programs shift to other facilities

Electric lights were still novel enough to make the news.

There was an "anti-cigarette league" because a "great many of the boys are addicted to it." The heated "natatorium" (swimming pool) was a wonder, holding 70,000 gallons of water "so clear…that a 10-cent piece laying on the bottom is magnified to the size of a half-dollar." And Col. Lyman B. Goff, the Pawtucket Boys' Club founder and principal philanthropist, handed over 400 shares of Pennsylvania Railway stock to start an endowment.

When the original Pawtucket Boys' Club opened its doors in 1902, Col. Goff's dream building was state of the art.

But 103 years later, antiquated systems, safety concerns, strict new fire codes, and rehabilitations estimated to exceed $500,000 doomed the building to mothballs. The recommendation to close the Club's oldest facility was approved in December by the board of directors.

Closing the building won't change programming, however. Programs for the 600 teens who used 53 East Avenue have already moved either to the Club's Arts Center a few doors away or to the Elson Branch on School Street.

A club for "unhappy boys"

"The club is designed for unhappy boys," speaker Thomas Chew said at its dedication, as the *Pawtucket Times* reported in July 1902. Boys Clubs were a relatively new phenomenon, meant for the cities, "designed to fight the street for the possession of the boy, that it might save him from vice, from crime and prison," said Chew.

Unhappy boys were those "who have little or no chance to see and hear the best things. The drunkard's child; the fatherless or motherless boy; the dull boy; the poor boy; the shiftless, the lazy, the cigarette fiend…the bad boy. Here they will all find a welcome."

Mr. Chew compared bad boys to that other "delicate piece of mechanism," a watch.

"If I were to put a sign on this building, so that every passer-by could tell what was being done within, it would be this: 'Boys Cleaned, Regulated and Repaired.'"

In 1923, boys line up at 53 East Avenue, the Club's original building.

Illustration 4 - Boys & Girls of Pawtucket News

Challenge Grants...continues

athletics; tutoring (Pawtucket's high school graduation rate is 67%, second lowest in Rhode Island); career counseling for teens; an intensely popular arts program; even hot meals.

Membership costs the child just $30. Yet some Pawtucket families have trouble affording even that modest amount. Nearly half of Pawtucket's children live in single-parent households. Almost a quarter of the city's kids live in poverty (versus 7% statewide).

"Who you calling a baby?"

New Baby Boom hits Pawtucket Club -- only this time it's 6 to 8 year olds

- Youngest member group grows 209% in just one year
- "The younger you get them, the better," comments Jim Hoyt, Pawtucket Club CEO

It's raining kids in Pawtucket. And they're really young.

In 2003, the Boys & Girls Club of Pawtucket welcomed 179 members ages 6 to 8.

In 2004, that number jumped 209%, as 554 members ages 6 to 8 participated in Club activities.

This bulge heralds more growth for the Club. It also puts additional pressure on facilities already stretched to accommodate the migration from the Teen Center.

The Boys & Girls Club of Pawtucket
One Moeller Place, Pawtucket, RI 02860
phone 401-722-8840
www.bgcpawt.org

New Hampshire couple invests in Pawtucket kids' potential

"Why my wife and I chose to make our largest charitable contribution ever, to the Boys & Girls Club of Pawtucket."

- Bottom line, says Pawtucket Club alum, since the community reaps the benefits, "it is up to us to pay for the services that the Club provides."

Anthony Ruddy spoke at our annual meeting on November 24 about why he and his wife, Lisa Baumgarten, residents of New Hampshire, pledged their largest-ever charitable gift to a Boys & Girls Club in Pawtucket.

"I grew up here in Pawtucket. I'm a second generation alumnus of the Boys & Girls Club. Both my mother and father were involved with the Club as children. And my father was not only a member, but worked five days a week at the East Avenue Branch through the 1940s and 50s.

"My sister and I became members of the Boys & Girls Club at the Elson Branch and joined the swim team with Jim Hoyt as coach and aquatics director. Over the years Jim has been coach, mentor, and friend.

"As business people, my wife and I look at philanthropy as investments. We look at organization and leadership. The Boys & Girls Club of Pawtucket excels in both of those areas.

"Although the Club is a non-profit entity, it must run as a business. But unlike a regular business, it offers a service - at a loss. You heard Phil [Ayoub] and Jim [Hoyt] say that it costs $1,000 per child, yet the Club charges $30 per child. That may seem like a strange business model, but make note...the children are not the customers of the Club - it is us, the community. We reap the benefits of the services the Club provides...by helping our children in need excel to their greatest potential, to secure their future. The Club does this with after-school programs, sports activities, tutoring, mentoring, and preparing our teenagers for college. The Club gives children a place to go, in a society where many children come home to an empty house during the day.

"The Club has met the challenges of a changing community, by changing with it. But the financial needs of the Club are greater than ever. As the community, it is up to us to pay for the services that the Club provides."

You can support the Pawtucket Boys & Girls Club through your company's United Way workplace campaign.

It's easy: Simply write in our agency name and address on your United Way pledge form. And thanks!

Celebrating the Offer

The following illustrations show elements from "Feeding the Hungry," the donor newsletter of Food for the Hungry (based in Phoenix, Arizona; operating worldwide). "Feeding the Hungry" is extraordinarily effective at raising more money from existing donors.

This "best practice" newsletter passionately links donors to a worldwide, world-changing mission. In this particular issue you'll see a perfect example of "celebrating the offer," in this case a 20:1 matching gift program. (*Writer: Joey Scanapico. Designer: Mike Gamble. Consultant: Domain Group. Used by permission of Food for the Hungry and the Domain Group.*)

Illustration 5 - Feeding the Hungry

This offer is so incredibly rich – "Every gift multiplies 20 times" – that it's worth introducing right on the envelope.

Jeff Brooks of the Domain Group also notes: "Every envelope should carry the message 'Newsletter Enclosed!' It will differentiate this piece from other types of mail. And remember, donors want newsletters. The thumbnail of the newsletter also advertises the unique content."

Illustration 6 - Feeding the Hungry

USAID Matching Grant brings Good News to world's poor

More lives will be saved as every $1 gift becomes $20

Finally, some good news for people who are suffering around the world ...

This month, because of a special Matching Grant we received from the United States Agency for International Development (USAID), your gift multiplies 20 times.

That's right: 20 times!

Every $1 you give becomes $20 in life-saving relief.

Do you know how many additional lives will be saved because of this offer? And how many will get to hear about Christ's love for the very first time? Literally thousands!

What a blessing, especially to people like 70-year-old Sori Harsama!

Mr. Harsama lives in Marsabit, a community in arid, remote northern Kenya. Four years ago, he could barely feed his wife and six children — mostly because of the way he was planting crops on his land.

Like most peasant farmers in the region, he didn't rotate his crops, didn't use fertilizer

Because of your kindness, many will hear about Christ for the very first time.

Because of your gift — and the USAID Matching Grant — thousands of lives will find true hope!

and didn't pay much attention to soil erosion. He depended on rain to water his crops — in a region that sees very little rain.

Not surprisingly, the soil became so unhealthy, nothing would grow in it anymore.

When Food for the Hungry first met Mr.

Harsama, he was looking for a new plot of land to grow food. We showed him how he could use the land he already had and make it fertile again with just a few changes.

Like using manure, adding irrigation to help with soil conservation and putting up a fence to protect his crops from

grazing livestock nearby. We even built a special fence to keep elephants away.

The changes worked so well that Mr. Harsama now grows enough to feed his family, and a little extra to sell for additional family income.

"I appreciate the

(continued on back page)

The offer is repeated and highlighted on the front cover, in the subhead of the lead story. Jeff Brooks again: "As the headline writers of the supermarket tabloids know, a subhead can create even more interest in the story."

Illustration 7 - Feeding the Hungry

Your gifts — and Food for the Hungry's expertise — are bringing a healthier lifestyle (along with God's Word) to hurting people everywhere.

USAID ... *(continued from page 1)*

nutritional supplements that my children get from the fruits and vegetables that are now planted on our land," he notes.

But that's not even the best part. With additional training from Food for the Hungry, Mr. Harsama has also become a leading advocate for better health in his village. Now he's encouraging his neighbors to set aside their cultural beliefs and start using latrines to fight the spread of disease.

"This training has changed my life completely," he says.

In a few short years, Mr. Harsama has gone from struggling peasant farmer to village leader. From using old, inefficient farming methods to utilizing new ways to grow healthy crops that are helping his family and his community. From hearing about God to seeing God work in his life, a fact that has caused his own faith to grow quickly.

Your gifts — and Food for the Hungry's expertise — are bringing a

healthier lifestyle (along with God's Word) to hurting people everywhere.

And this month — because of a special Matching Grant from USAID — your gift goes even further.

Twenty times further!

The poor can't wait a minute longer. Please send a generous gift today. And watch your kindness begin to change the world.

Starting with people like Mr. Harsama.

Use the enclosed Matching Grant Check to multiply your gift 20 times to help others.

1 Fill in the amount you want to have multiplied.

2 Write out your own personal check for your gift amount.

3 Enclose your personal check along with the reply form.

Your gift, when combined with the USAID Matching Grant, will provide 20 times as much help for suffering men, women and children around the world.

This particular issue of the newsletter is pretty much about a single topic: the "$1 becomes $20" offer. No matter where you turn, the offer is repeated. Shown here: the back cover. Note that the bottom half has very explicit instructions explaining how to take advantage of the match. It even includes a picture of the reply device being slipped into the reply envelope (this is the "show" aspect of show-and-tell).

ACKNOWLEDGMENTS

This is my favorite part to write in the whole book: my thanks.

I've had years of encouragement. At the front of that line, I have to put Harvey McKinnon, Mal Warwick and my wife-colleague-best friend, Simone Joyaux. Simone and I talk about fundraising many times a day and love our life among nonprofits. She long ago became an author and coaxed me to catch up. Harvey and Mal lost no opportunity to point out how easy it is to write a book (they were lying, of course, but I appreciate their cheers and poms-poms).

I asked dozens of people to review this book and invited their frankest suggestions on how to make it better. Critics, I salute you. I weighed every comment. The published version reflects the sum total of your insights, course corrections, and oops-collecting. Lingering blemishes are my doing; you tried to warn me.

I prostrate myself with gratitude to all those who took the time. Naming names, in alpha order: Michael Beneke, Aimee Bott Joyaux, Lisa Bousquet, Ken Burnett, Jerry Cianciolo, Sarah Coviello, Steve Herlich, Jonathan Feist, Nisia Hanson, Kris Hermanns, Dianna Huff, Madeleine Langford-Allen, Pat Masterson, Harvey McKinnon, John C. Meyers, Ari Matusiak, Miriam May, Jerry Panas, Jim Rattray, Rick Schwartz, Beth Stafford, Mal Warwick, Ryan West.

From that crew, I want to thank especially Rick Schwartz. I was in my "can't see the forest for the trees" period. Rick spent days reorganizing my first draft so it would make more sense. He acted as the readers' surrogate and advocate, and as the author's friend. His clear thinking about structure guided me to a hugely improved second draft.

More special thanks to Jerry Panas, who recommended my writing to Jerry Cianciolo. A Jerry-to-Jerry-to-Tom triple play.

As for the final draft, the one you're holding in your hands: I owe unique thanks. Again, to Jerry Cianciolo. How do you measure the gratitude an author feels for a publisher who shows up unannounced and says "I want you"? Who is passionate about how-to books? (Me, too!) Whose editorial judgment is trustworthy, loyal, brave...and outstanding? He told me, "Our readers like short chapters." Short chapters it is.

I want to thank, too, the thousands of fundraisers who have come to my workshops. Many of you sent me your stuff for review in advance of a workshop, willing to share with the rest of the class, willing to risk my criticism. I have learned so much from your efforts and experiences and questions. This book is an attempt to pay that forward.

The information in this book was assembled from the bricks and mortar of many authorities and sources. A contemptibly incomplete list of those who taught me important things about communications (aside from several of the reviewers mentioned earlier) includes Bruce Bendinger, Robert Bly, Penelope Burk, John Caples, Dale Carnegie, Barbara G. Ellis, Stephen Hitchcock, Jerry Huntsinger, Roland Kuniholm, Kay Partney Lautman, Herschell Gordon Lewis, David Ogilvy, Ellis Robinson, Colin Wheildon, Roy H. Williams. I know all of these people from their books. Their generous, plain-talking, entertaining books.

I use your lessons every day.

Big Gifts for Small Groups

A Board Member's 1-Hour Guide to Securing Gifts
of $500 to $5,000 • *Andy Robinson*

If yours is among the tens of thousands of organizations for whom six- and seven-figure gifts are unattainable, then *Big Gifts for Small Groups* is just the ticket for you and your board.

Robinson is the straightest of shooters. There literally isn't one piece of advice in this book that's glib or inauthentic. As a result, board members will instantly take to the book, confident the author isn't slinging easy bromides.

They'll learn everything they need to know from this one-hour read: how to get ready for the campaign, whom to approach, where to find them; where to conduct the meeting, what to bring with you, how to ask, how to make it easy for the donor to give, what to do once you have the commitment – even how to convey your thanks in a memorable way.

Fundraising Mistakes that Bedevil All Boards

A 1-Hour Guide to Identifying and Overcoming
Obstacles to Your Success • *Kay Sprinkel Grace*

Fundraising mistakes are a thing of the past. Or, rather, there's no excuse for making a mistake anymore. And that goes for board members, staff, novice, or veteran.

If you blunder from now on, it's simply evidence you haven't read Kay Sprinkel Grace's book, *Fundraising Mistakes that Bedevil All Boards (and Staff Too)*, in which she exposes *all* of the costly errors that thwart us time and again. The appeal of this book is that in one place it gathers and discusses the "Top 40" miscues – some readily apparent, others more subtle.

Just as anyone involved in journalism should own a copy of Strunk and White's, *The Elements of Style*, anyone involved in fundraising – board member, staff, volunteer – should have *Fundraising Mistakes that Bedevil All Boards (and Staff Too)* by their side.

How Are We Doing?

A 1-Hour Guide to Evaluating Your Performance
as a Nonprofit Board • *Gayle L. Gifford*

Until now, almost all books dealing with board evaluation have had an air of unreality about them. The perplexing graphs, the matrix boxes, the overlong questionnaires. It took only a thumbing through to render a judgment: "My board's going to use this? Get real!"

Enter Gayle Gifford. Inhale the fresh air. See the ground break. Watch the clutter clear. This nationally respected trainer has pioneered an elegantly simple and enjoyable way for your board to evaluate *and* improve its overall performance.

It all comes down to answering a host of straightforward questions – questions that as Graham Greene would say, get to "the heart of the matter."

INDEX

American Civil Liberties Union, 20

Associated Press Stylebook and Libel Manual, 79

Barna, George, 13

Barna Research Group, 13

Bohnsack, John R. (Paster John), 56, 105

Boys & Girls Club of Pawtucket, 106, 115-116

Burk, Penelope, 108

Brookings Institution, 22

Campbell, Bruce, 23

Carnegie, Dale, 63

Chronicle of Philanthropy, The, 22

Clean Water Action, 49-50

Community Emergency Service, 56, 105

Conservator, 50

Conservation Law Foundation, 51

Copy-Editing and Headline Handbook, The, 73, 91

Desktop Publishing by Design, 79

Dewey, John, 63

Domain Group, The, 104, 112-113

Donor-Centered Fundraising, 108

Ducks Unlimited Canada, 50

Ellis, Barbara G., 73, 91

Edmonton Alberta SPCA, 101

Flesch-Kincaid scale, 83

Free-range Thinking, 50

Freud, Sigmund, 63

Garcia, Mario R., 87

Goodman, Andy, 50

Gossage, Howard Luck, 42

Green Door, 109

Hospice of the Chesapeake, 101

How to Win Friends and Influence People, 63

Jung, Carl, 25

Lant, Jeffrey, 105

Maclean's, 45

Manchester (Ct) Area Conference of Churches, 63

McKinnon, Harvey, 70

Myers-Briggs test, 24

National Parks Conservation Association, 51

Newsweek, 81

Panas, Jerry, 13

Planned Parenthood, 20

Redesigning Print for the Web, 87

Rhode Island Community Food Bank, 37

Rule of Seven, 105

Russ Reid Co., The, 13

Seattle Children's Theatre, 109-110

Southcoast, 53-54

Stafford, Beth, 63

Type & Layout, 70

United Negro College Fund, 52

Vogele, Siegfried, 65, 67-68

Wall Street Journal, The, 44-45, 59-60, 83, 91, 95

Warwick, Mal, 22, 70

Wheildon, Colin, 70

Worsley Press, 70-71

Wylie, Ann, 92

Copies of this book, and others from the publisher,
are available at discount when purchased in quantity
for boards of directors, volunteers, or staff.

Emerson
& Church
PUBLISHERS

P.O. Box 338 • Medfield, MA 02052
Tel. 508-359-0019 • Fax 508-359-2703
www.emersonandchurch.com